ABOUT THE SIZE OF IT

Poetry by Tom Disch

Highway Sandwiches, 1970
(*with Charles Platt and Marilyn Hacker*)

The Right Way to Figure Plumbing, 1972

ABCDEFG HIJKLM NPOQRST UVWXYZ, 1981

Burn This, 1982

Orders of the Retina, 1982

Here I Am, There You Are, Where Were We, 1984

Yes, Let's: New and Selected Poems, 1989

Dark Verses and Light, 1991

Haikus of an AmPart, 1991

The Dark Old House, 1996

Poetry Criticism

The Castle of Indolence, 1994
On Poetry, Poets, and Poetasters

The Castle of Perseverance, 2002
Job Opportunities in Contemporary Poetry

Tom Disch
About the Size of It

ANVIL PRESS POETRY

Published in 2007
by Anvil Press Poetry Ltd
Neptune House 70 Royal Hill London SE10 8RF
www.anvilpresspoetry.com

This book is published with financial assistance
from Arts Council England

Designed and set in Monotype Bembo by Anvil
Printed and bound in England
by Cromwell Press, Trowbridge, Wiltshire

ISBN 978 0 85646 391 4

A catalogue record for this book
is available from the British Library

Contents

ACKNOWLEDGEMENTS

Grateful acknowledgement is made to the editors of the following in which these poems have appeared:

"Centennial Tankas", "Dialogue with a Spider", "The Mushrooms' Salon", "The Rapture": *After/Lives*; "The Last Time I Saw Paris": *American Scholar*; "The Size of the World": *Annual Survey of American Poetry 1985*, Poetry Anthology Press; "A": *bellevue broadside*; "In Memoriam": *Best American Poetry 1989*, Scribner's; "The Crumbling Infrastructure": *Best American Poetry 1990*, Scribner's; "Buying a Used Car", "A Centenary Observation", "Coming To", "In Memoriam", "Indian Spring", "Juliet, Voice Over", "Not Quite a Sonnet But I Love You Just the Same", "October", "September", "Slouches", "Waking Early New Year's Day, Without a Hangover": *Boulevard*; "At the Van Gogh Museum", "Class Notes", "The Flesh's Wedding", "A Galop for Cesar Franck", "Gods", "In a Time of Plagues", "Inventory", "Systems of Mourning", "A War Memorial", "Womankind and Poesy": *Chronicles*; "Haikus of an AmPart": *Coffee House chapbook*; "'Ritin'": *Crosscurrents*; "Fashion Statements": *Fashion and Fragrance*; "Duelling Platitudes", "The Thought That Counts": *Grand Street*; "The Hawk and the Metaphor": Aralia Press keepsake; "The Cubist Paints of Lesser Museums": *Inquiry*; "The Last Shows of Summer": *Lake Street Review*; "A Benevolent Villanelle", "Birdsong Interpreted", "Sylvan Marriage": *Light*; "Nightmare on Elm Street": *New Republic*; "Songs of the Rooftops": *Open Places*; "The Dirt and the Willow": *Paris Review*; "The Dot on the i", "Medusa at Her Vanity", "Red Tulips in 1947", "Remarks Concerning the Fitness of All Things", "The Return to Nature", "A Stroll Through Moscow", "Three People and Their Feelings", "To the Young Mercenaries", "Villanelle for Charles Olson": *Poetry*; "Colloquy": *SF Eye*; "A Gravedigger's Soliloquy", "Ode to Equanimity", "Rules of Order for New Conservatives", "Theseus to Hippolyta": *Salmagundi*; "A Cape Mendocino Rose": *Sequoia*; "After Péguy", "Gilda: an Entr'acte", "Symphonic Ode for St. Cecilia's Day", "Yorick's Reply": *Shenandoah*; "The Crumbling Infrastructure", "We Are Divided Everywhere in Two Parts": *Southwest Review*; "Summer of '88", "The Varieties of Oneiric Experience": *Tampa Review*; "Mahler's 8th": *Theology Today*; "The Book in Your Hand", "Nether: a Traveller's Notes", "The Size of the World", "The Squirrel", "A Treatise on the Common Cold", "The Vindication of Obesity": *Times Literary Supplement*; "Rocks on a Winter Evening": *Velocities*; "Jerusalem Recaptured": *Western Humanities Review*; "Brief Lives", "Death Wish IV": *Witness*; "Riddle": *Yale Review*

I

About the Size of It

The Dot on the i

They mean so much, these little things:
The way as it sinks into lower-case
The aristocratic I loses its
Ionic capital to wear the unassuming
Livery that it alone of all the letters
Must be humbled by. Yet it is wise in that
By doing so it intimates of what Pope hints at
When he speaks of mankind's middling state
Between the macro- and the microscopic –
An idea too easily dismissed as out-of-date,
As though the only units of time worth noticing
Were those with the eternal rondures
Of our O's. But what is this O but
A dot with a hole in it? Wherein
Other dots may blossom into other O's,
A rose of infinite regressions like
The marvelous Mandelbrot transformations
Illustrated so beguilingly in a recent
Scientific American. When it comes to the sense
Of beauty we are all Pythagoreans,
Transfixed upon the ineffable and inexplicable
Significance of a number; for instance
(Or especially?), *i*, the square root of minus-one.
Or think of 'quantum leaps,' by which in common usage
We refer to movements of momentous scale
But which in fact are minuscule, beyond the reach
Of measurement. High and low, the infinite
And the inconsiderable, merge in the Arctic
Paradiso, Number, where, you guessed it, Number One
Is the great revolving flywheel generating
All numbers else, except its negation. Think of
It, and think as well of those teeny tiny lovely touches
That so enrich each individual existence:
Peter Sellers' telling tics in his role as

Dr. Strangelove, the pepper polka-dotting an egg,
The leg of a dog lifted to piss – all this
And indefinitely more, for it is an aspect
Of the limitless extent of all single particulars
That it includes more than one, than anyone,
Can specify. Just try it. And it is this
Limitlessness of all that is little that allows
A theoretic possibility of a plenum
Coextensive with the mind and reach of each
Man and woman alive, and unalive, of absolutely
Everyone, in a democracy of dust where even the largest
Integer is a function of the number one, and may
Be laid low by i. Incredible, isn't it?
I love you, and that's equally incredible,
Equally axiomatic. Shall we stop there,
Or proceed to the next coulisse down the road?
We'll stop there. I love you. That's it.

A

letter opens
to release
its quantum
of silence

sporelike
it swells
into the space
between adjoining
words

becomes
a margin

then
an entire room
of silences
that face each other
calmly as mourners
at the death
of an indifferent friend

it eases
out the window
into the stateliness
of a high
penumbral column
that glides
in a motion
strictly parallel
to the fuselage
and wings
above

darkening leaves
whipping over hills
touching the Atlantic
in an almost endless
caress
slowly altering
in its obliquity as
the moving earth
and stationary sun
align themselves
toward a shadowless
evening

when
all its mammoth bulk
condenses to
a jot
of emptiness
no bigger than
the snug triangle
again atop
the letter

A

The Thought That Counts

as though a light had gone on

the thought that counts
suddenly was conscious

and thought of the numbers
from one to ten,
each number higher than the one

or two or three before,
a fact the thought that counted
chose to ignore:
for these were not apples or oranges,

they were not even the names
of all the registered atoms
in the universe,
but rather the address
of the registration office itself,

where an endless flux
of elemental mush
waited in long, long, long lines
to get their visas
for existence and the privilege
of being particular,

a privilege we who possess it
are too liable to take for granted,
just as we tend to forget
the enormousness of virtually everything:
the long highways so variously numbered,

the fleets of licensed vans
bearing invoiced boxes of grapefruits

for tomorrow's breakfast, tomorrow being
the eighth and a good morning for
a grapefruit, as indeed what morning is not,
for its proper preparation affords us
the first periodicitous paradigm
of the day, as our knives slip
along its radii and we think,
along with the thought that counts,

not of any individual grapefruit
in our hands but of the grapefruit
single as the sun
that burns its identifying brand
on the mind's eye: one,
and one again, and still one
more – what idea could be
as pure? as sweetly apt
to bear repeating:

one
and one
and then one more
and then another one
and so on for
as long as one can,
in cadence with the count
of the thought that is counting
the numbers from one to ten, and then
onwards: it is as though . . .

as though a light had gone on,
as though the thought that counts
suddenly were conscious
and were to think of the numbers from one

to ten, each number higher than the one
preceding, a fact we may choose
to ignore, for these are not apples or oranges,
not even the names of all that is numerable
in the universe but rather the address
to which one sends each issue of a serial
that always ends: (to be continued)

The Size of the World

To say it is enormous, or to search the thesaurus
For synonyms to its immensity will not express
The size of it. It dwarfs all our opinions
And knowledge, and even when we try to expand
Our vocabulary to take in the latest large
Idea, such as superstrings or ecology
Or the transcending of this or that category,
We are only inventing new conventions.
Something is left out in even the best new schema:
There is no room for happiness
Or the Holy Family on Xmas Eve
Or the price of eggs or something else so significant
That without it all the rest is vanity.
Nor is there any wisdom in such an admission;
It is as a watercolor of the ocean
To the ocean itself. But this can be a source
Of joy, or, lacking that, of a sweet and needful
Self-deception, a safety exit
To practical faith, not one connected
To what may be known but only to what may not.
This is the realm poetry particularly
Inhabits, the teasing out of thought
Into pleasing shapes, coiffing the minds
Of a happy few to some provisory accommodation
To their ignorance – without euphoria,
Without unfounded hope, and yet enchanted.
Oh, it is a realm isolate as Moctezuma's,
And, some have said, forlorn. But vivider,
For all that, than the actual universe
In which we bulk so small, and which impinges
Every split-second even on these complacent
Maunderings, suggesting other combinations,
More refined adaptions to the fact
Of all facts, the set of all sets, the sum

Of all summery days, when the sun shines
With Platonic brightness and the mind is inclined
To lazily number the ways I love you, and the cause
Of it: To wit, because you're fair, because
We've been together since the dawn of time, because
You're so fine a backseat driver, or because
You've got a way with words, mine *and* yours.
By such means – poetry, love, what have you –
The universe can be contained, the world
Reduced to a manageable mass
Where superstrings may coexist
With the atoms of Democritus, though we know
All the while the world is larger
Than all these transcripts of our idle chatter.
Some things matter more than others: mothers
More than Coca-Cola, pigeons more than fleas.
Yet even these neglected categories
May abound in unthought possibilities.
Life's so rich, and life's only a part of it:
There are, as well, minerals and large machines,
Bricks and various gases – and, if *The Times* is right,
Six entirely new dimensions, ten
In all, and we may be, in every one,
A kind of sun unto our constituent
Genes, and our Roy Rogers too, a meaty
Stew of recombinant nuances;
Cities built, and histories, meals cooked,
Books read, scenes viewed, drawers opened and closed,
Glimpsed lovelinesses and horrors, which in
Some larger perspective, some stricter mind's
Accounting, are as the blow that ended
Tamburlaine and not of immediate importance.
Though, who knows, without some particular
Forgotten warlord we might not be here to share
This evanescing afternoon of broken-
Bottled pavements and friendly endlessness,
Friendly because no one cares. So life's a scream,

So what? What are we doing when we talk
Like this, unlistened to, a ballpoint
Pressed against the ruled paper's tenderness?

The Vindication of Obesity

I

After the satieties of summer, the amplitude
Of autumn, and winter's grasping
For the last calories of warmth and cake
Comes the season of penitence.
We wear drab colors then and comb our hair
Differently. We weigh ourselves
On trustworthy scales whose unwavering needles
Accuse us of gross excesses. No one so fat
Will ever be initiate to the gnosis
Of fitness nor share the normal human experience
Of paradise. Our only hope then
Lies in diet and expiation, our only happiness
Those tasteless ikons everywhere advertising
The pleasures of fully resurrected flesh.

Within the bobbling, semi-solid fat we feel
The incipient musculature, the ridges
Of the unseen ribcage, the wistful lungs,
The heart, so trusted and abused, the scapegoat
Glands, the coiling bowels — all of it still intact
And waiting, like South America, to be set free.

And so our horrid hulk heaves up
From its recliner to stuff itself
Defiantly into its casings, thence
To the gymnasium for another taxing episode
In the decline of one's personal Empire.

Well met, Trimalchio! You've gained some weight.

2

Fat, though never beautiful, may yet be proud.
Gibbon, Aquinas, several famous comedians,
Even Lord Buddha – all were complacently obese.
They lived before the fatal Scarsdale diet,
When wisdom had immense vested interests
And dared to smile at the vernal excellings
Of the slim. What is it all for, that
Gauntness, those lissome arms, torsos rippled
Into breastplates – what but war?
Once, however, one's declared
Hors de combat, there's no need to clank about
In armor. Let Hotspur and Hal dispute
The relative allure of their tights and doublets;
We, Falstaff, will settle for a pint of ale
Snug in a dark booth at the back of the bar,
Dipping our hands into perpetually replenished
Bowls of peanuts, exchanging recipes.

Omnia Accipimus, our motto, means
There is no food, however ominous,
We won't omnivorously devour: flesh
Of frogs, of eels, of foetuses; cheeses rank
As death; eggs, seeds, sprouts, fungi,
Whatever promise of growth we can divert
To our own swollen purposes. We lick our lips
And lift our glasses to the clods
And huntsmen whose *raison d'être* we are –
Long may they delve and slaughter!

3

Hal speaks:

Old man, put by
This self-expensive merriment. Feel the pinch
Of your trousers and not your desires'.
Recognise that pig in the mirror
As a mortal enemy. Feed it nothing
But scorn till it confesses
Itself to be the new, ameliorated you.
Deed those needless fifty pounds
To a deserving tailor, geriatric
Specialists, a grateful posterity.

Falstaff replies:

Enough, dear lad. A great posterior's
The cause we serve who live in hope
Not of crowns but coronaries.
Do not you know that, like the swan,
Even the carefullest eater soon enough dies?
Why then, how then, resist the dreadful
Evening's neon solace, EAT? Say I removed
These wreaths of fat to vaunt the shapely
Cranium beneath – how would that benefit
Your commonwealth, my liege? Shall every bar
And bakery give way to studios
Of dance and martial arts? Shall I subsist
On Perrier and salad greens? No wine! no bread!
Nor even salt, because my heart, for reasons
Of its own, will not keep pace with my ingestive
Genius. No, Falstaff defies your regimens!
He eats, he drinks, and merrily repeats
The process tomorrow and tomorrow and tomorrow.

Meanwhile tonight, just down the street,
I know a restaurant that serves
Wines of inexpressible immodesty.

Such peppers in oil, such onions in cream,
Such breasts of capon in Sauce Supreme!
I can also recommend the *bœuf en daube*,
Sweetbreads, *pasta putanesca*, squab . . .

4

No need to listen to Gargantua
Ruminating old menus. That tongue will wag
Until it gets a bone. Instead, let's pan
Across the wider world and measure man.
From suckers born every minute to old farts
Drooling Fixodent, behold the classic span
Whose broad curve encloses all waistlines
Whatsoever: the innocence of 28;
The initial twinges rounding the bend to 32;
Then 36, when mirrors are banished for their lies;
The reckless shame of 44, no stopping now,
It's 50 next, and horrors even more
Unspeakable, until at last all waists
Are wasted in the toilet of the tomb,
While our immortal parts (as some believe)
Swell beyond measurement and rise
To glory coextensive with the sky's,
Where, eternally obese, our Saints appear
In Levis larger than the troposphere.
Such are the sizes all men fit, and such
The consequence of eating far too much.

5

But seriously, Doc, am I to blame?
As much as any box of Cheerios
I am the product of Big Businesses,
For whom I loyally, compulsively
Consume. Before my infant gums
Had budded teeth, *they* tempted me

With honeyed words and sugared slops
Dyed to those colors research proves
Would sureliest deprave and addict.
Hyperkinetically I bolted down
Each landscape of meat and potatoes
Questing the grail of dessert,
And it was there, among those modulated sweets,
My ravished tongue first learned to speak,
Schooled by paradigms of silverware,
Cooking triads *à la* Levi-Strauss,
My mother's wit and father's Polonian
Commend of cliché: a happy childhood,
And not unrepresentative. I throve,
Converting calories to play
And, a few years later, to ballet. I burned
With fevers of caffeine, relaxed
In baths of alcohol, and survived
The intervals of foodlessness by smoking Kents.

This was the wisdom of our tribe
(One of the largest in Minnesota),
The Over-reaching, Over-achieving Over-eaters.
Now, with 40 years behind me in the OOO,
It would be folly to repent. Of what?
Those honey-saturated hours in the hive
Are sweet to memory still. Doubtless
I'll continue to observe certain equinoctial
Dietary rites, but when I diet it will be
In the service of my tongue
That old recidivist, that it may eat
More immoderately when I am thin.

Reverting briefly to the matter of
Man's first temptation and fall from grace,
I must in fairness exculpate
General Foods, *et al.* Adam didn't sin
Because Eve tempted him: he *chose* to eat

That apple. He might – we each might – have refused.
But once having bitten, no sinner could wish
Never to have known, never to have been
Involved and implicated in the dialectic actions
Of that flesh, which, in its complex
Disintegrations, informs each hungry pore
With news of the deliciousness of death.

Red Tulips in 1947

It lasts so long, bulks so large,
Exists in such high resolution
You think you might learn to like it
Once you got used to the silence,
The innocuous cuisine, the endless recycling
Of the garbagey past, for Eternity
Is only here and now on tap forever,
Exactly as that middlebrow fabulist Wilder
Imagined, each frame amenable to my summons,
Tame as a home movie, but with this difference,
That I can feel only what I felt
The first time round, the same
Small envies, stale longueurs, exasperations;
The same fretfulness, as when
On a Thursday morning in 1947,
Having finished with the paper, I looked out
The kitchen window at a flower bed –
Not ours, a neighbor's – and watched red petals
Jittering in the wind. Those tulips
I didn't see at all; rather, my frayed nerves
Found in them their own reflection, and now
Again, revisiting the scene, they are
My mirror and sympathetic fallacy;
Scentless, senseless soul's amber,
Which I view and review like some minimum-
Wage security guard patrolling an empty store,
Video screen by video screen, from his post
Before a basement wall of monitors. Yet he is not
Entirely bored, for see – on one screen
He can watch the tape he made a week ago,
No sound track, no credits, just two pelvises
In sync and lipstick the color of these tulips
Still fresh this Thursday morning of my afterlife.

II

Love and Death

A Centenary Observation

I was young once – so were you.
Youth is when we think we'll do
Wonders someday. That day comes
With remainders more than sums.

You were young once – so was I.
That can make me want to cry
For all we've lost. But that's okay:
While the sun shined we made hay.

He was young once – weren't we all?
Now it's his centennial,
And every word he wrote is Writ,
His very postcards English Lit.

The moral of this? That life is brief,
The laurel a most belated leaf,
And youth a wine that doesn't keep.
Before it sours, lads, drink deep.

Duelling Platitudes

Because it is an imperative voiced
    in the accents of ancestors
    otherwise unremembered,

Gather ye rosebuds while ye may
    carries a proverbial force
    that makes us pay attention.

Only the dead may address us as 'ye.'
    But where are these rosebuds?
    Are they cheap as the hay

We're to make while the sun shines?
    What penalties and fines
    can we expect to pay

If we're caught in the act of gathering
    someone else's rosebuds?
    Ancestral voices disagree

On these issues, and we must choose
    our authorities carefully;
    one false step and there is

A piper to pay, and who knows how much
    a piper requires
    when the fat's in the fire?

Eat, drink, and be merry: okay,
    but will you still love me
    when I'm old and gray?

Which brings us to the Middle Way,
    another idea
    old as those hills

Where rosebuds are rare as a day
    in June and pipers play
    another tune –

Love's old sweet song, maybe,
    or other golden oldies
    from the age of the Golden Mean.

Songs are seldom what they seem;
    the sirens who charm us
    may suddenly scream

Rape!, and words can harm us
    as brutally as sticks and stones.
    It depends on our tone.

A queen who tells us to eat cake
    may be making
    a big mistake,

But the same advice from our corner baker
    is par for the course,
    not grounds for divorce.

All adages are relative; each
    will have its season.
    So dare to eat your peach,

My friend, but keep it within reason.

The Flesh's Wedding

It is with the flesh, as with moat other marriages,
That a time comes, a middle age, when the bond loosens.
Not a divorce, necessarily – fondness may persist –
But there is not that knot of simple union
That appetite ties in our honeymoon years.
We begin to get fat in a different way than we got fat
In our pococurante thirties, when, however much
We ate or entertained, we still worried
About waistlines and went to a gym. Now we know it's no use.
We have become painfully aware of all the ways our flesh
Betrays us, and those who can afford the preposterous fees
Begin to visit exotic professionals – peridontists,
Plastic surgeons, barbers with a sideline in toupees.
The divorced often seem to suffer less,
But you will notice how many of them become alcoholics
And smoke like chimneys, clandestine anchorites
Flagellating livers, lungs, and hearts in lieu of
Spouses lost. The happiest are those who've never wed,
Who always recognized flesh as an encumbrance
Or simply didn't recognize it and jetted ahead,
Snug in the 747s of pure reasonableness, sipping
The vile complimentary wine, oblivious of everything
But the fluffy clouds below and the books in their laps.

The Ferris Wheel

At first we were delighted when the man at the controls
Seemed to lose track of who'd already gone round
And who hadn't and gave us a second ride for free.
Whee! we thought. Here we go again. First,
The stepwise ascent, the car rocking at each pause,
The view enlarging, until at the very top
We could see beyond the midway and the fairgrounds,
Across the dark August treetops, all the way
To the 1st National Bank. Then, the last batch
Of ticket holders being settled in their swaying seats,
The quick unsettling backwards descent,
The swoop upwards, outwards, above the lookers-
And the cheerers-on – supportive parents,
Jealous sibs, and the people waiting in line,
Already imagining themselves as us. Around
We went and up and down in a motion no longer
Queasy-making but easy and agreeable. We were
Becoming habitues and connoisseurs of the unusual
But ever-recurring vistas, trying to equate
The notches of the skyline with the known
Geometries of highways and streets. But when,
A second time, our car whisked past the wooden exit
Platform, we'd had enough, and I shouted down
At the ponytailed incompetent in charge of things,
'Hey, how about us?' Too late, we were already
Rising on high. You said, 'I don't believe this.'
'Unreal,' I agreed. 'But I guess we'll just have to
Relax and enjoy it.' Somehow that wasn't possible.
Each time as our car swept down to perigee
I tried to catch the attention of our insentient
Tormentor, whose face, each time, was turned away.
'Hey you with the tattoos!' He didn't hear,
Or wouldn't, but preened his carnival flesh

Before a pair of teddy-bear-toting teenagers
Behind the barrier, while we continued to revolve
In our fixed orbit, Ixions of the State Fair.
A fourth go-round, and then a fifth. Four cars ahead
Were empty now, and three immediately behind,
And he pretended ours was empty, too. We cried out
To the people on the ground, 'We can't get off!
Please tell that man to –' But already we'd been
Whirled up and out of earshot. The few who
Noticed us would smile and wave, or pantomime
A funhouse version of our panic. By now
We were more furious than fearful. But what to do?
That's when you took off your Land's End
Red silk turtleneck and used it as a semaphore,
And I stood up, legs braced against the safety bar,
Unzipped, and took a pee. And I will tell you this:
Until you've pissed from a revolving
Ferris wheel, you don't know what life is.

Not Quite a Sonnet But I Love You Just the Same

They sing almost the same song every night,
And daylong too, the thrushes of this place.
So beautiful! So beautiful, and true,
Though I've no paraphrase for what they say.
Yet surely it's more than the squallers' rights
Declared and redeclared by crows and jays.
Birds of that sort do what they have to do:
They grub for bugs and eat each other's fleas, —
But we are free and can sing what we please.
And if the song becomes familiar
Upon repeated hearing, is that a fault?
Truth bears repeating, or it is not truth.
We hum old melodies as deer lick salt.
They are both pleasures and necessities.
In middle age I love you, as in youth.

A Cape Mendocino Rose

Trapped in this single hope
That life goes on, life does go on,
We search for a suitable trope.

That life goes on, life does go on
Can't be denied, until it can.
'Gather ye rosebuds,' that dark koan

Expresses best, and earliest,
The search for a suitable trope.
Or there's old Horace G's 'Go west!'

Here on the Pacific coast
The sun spotlights a spectral rose.
Trapped in a single trope,
We lurch from hope to specious hope.

Riddle

Sometimes I seem the merest haze of good
Intentions, as when streaks of polish, missed
By a paper towel, form cloudy scripts
On the finish of the car, blemishes essentially
Overlookable. Then I take root, become
Intrinsic as the second, irregular frame
Of tarnish at a cheap mirror's edge, unsightly
Perhaps, but not yet an eyesore to the eye
That's fixed on its opposite number at
The mirror's equator. At last
Even with the carefulest adjustments of the glass
I can't be blinked away. I've come to stay,
A sty not only in the eye but reeking of pigshit
And bonded to the flesh of the prodigal come home
To roost, with no excuse, all his graces
Gone to seed, a garden that is all one weed.
Who am I? Oh, come on, you know my name.

Three People and Their Feelings

I

Trust was his friend with whom he'd play
    Peek-a-boo and Ride the Pony.
Warmth was a woman old and gray,
    And Resignation was her crony.

Sweetness was his favorite aunt
    And Jealousy his sibling.
Tenderness was full of cant
    And ever busy scribbling.

When I grow up, the infant thought,
    I'll be like them until I drop.
The boy was sold as he was bought,
    And now he is a traffic cop.

II

Love had moved to another coast;
    Her calls to him were all refused.
Sorrow was a parent's ghost,
    Pity a child who'd been abused.

While pallid Anger sat and stewed,
    Fear dogged her steps from street to street.
Joy rarely laughed (she thought it rude),
    And Ennui lived to overeat.

Every July her feelings met
    At a kind of family reunion,
And she would stay at home and get
    Drunk in blissful self-communion.

III

Desire had died and left no will,
    So Wistfulness now had to work.
Mirth survived on Pronestyl,
    But still he was the same dumb jerk.

Pain came each day at four o'clock
    To leave a bag of groceries.
Envy was proud she still could walk
    Despite the problem with her knees.

He seldom saw them anymore
    Except for Pain, and sometimes Grief.
He lived above a record store
    (Which doesn't matter if you're deaf).

A Treatise on the Common Cold

Neither the heart nor the liver are its source,
Nor yet the nerves except in the limiting sense
That all knowledge is a nervous affliction:
True pain is muscular and arises from
Immoral action. All germs and spirochaetae
Are merest messengers, whose immutable scrolls
Translate themselves instanter to
Dilations, tremblings, terror. This is not true,
Though it approximates a truth no tyrant dares
Entirely to disregard. All who have felt pain know
The respect in which it is deserved, just
As they can sense some converse innocence.
Fate is not fair: it is so. But we are not through –
Far from it! – with the soma. Much must be said
Of the precise distress attendant on
The annual anguish of the common cold:
How its first premonitions lie mute
At the back of the throat, a Yom Kippur
Demanding the tongue knows not what true
Confession, and thence its transit down
The tubes that bridge mind and matter
To lodge among the lungs and the lungs' associates
For a season long as Lent. A dismal guest –
Lazy, gluttonous, littering Kleenexes
And innuendoes vis-à-vis one's life
Expectancy. What is this little pea,
It wants to know, so close enclosed
In the soft matrix of the underarm?
What mean these deliquescent stools?
Like dear old Dixie's apocryphal troublemakers
From out of state, it jeers at the forces
Established to uphold order, peace, and ignorance.
Flesh, gaining consciousness, rebels

Against the mind's exactions. Forgotten
Scars grow livid and begin to itch.
The flaccid legs ache with the remembrance
Of how, long ago, at the price of a wish,
Compliant pipelines would open and a brighter blood
Would flow wherever desire felt a need or will required.
The diaphragm, like a corpse returned
Electrically to life, grabs
Whatever strings and tendons come to hand
And twangs on them with a rhapsode's abandon.
Only the docile fingers, the jesuitic lips
Resist, as best they can, the summons
To insurrection, turning pages,
Murmuring prayers, awaiting the hour
Of their re-elevation. That all these ills
Proceed like axioms from ancient usurpations
Is a fact they will not countenance,
Though the eyes, as they narrow, would seem to be
Sensible of every tissue's intricate complicity.

In Memoriam

Nothing, no one, gives me rest
I have put it to the test
And it is not an idle jest
The life I live must lead to death
An emptiness and end of breath
Though still my heart beats in my breast
Nothing, no one, gives me rest

The streets are filled with cryers crying
No end of them, nor yet of dying
Some men may smile a little while
If sellers sell and some are buying
But they will join the rank and file
Who decorate our ancient Nile
No end of them, nor yet of dying

Memorials are built and then
Time silts a river, builds a fen
And tells its immemorial jest
To the worst as to the best
The world will be as it has been
I am feeling so depressed
Nothing, no one, gives me rest

Yorick's Reply

The rub, Milord? Then, if you please, a bit
To the back. Yes, there, just where the mud
Has scabbed to it. But still I want to know:
The rub? Who ever forfeited his sleep
For fear of dreams? Dreams vary here on Earth,
And so they may hereafter. Why be perplexed?
Life is a dream, as I have heard, and if
Our death's another, may we well not hope
For dreams that correspond to what we wish?
I did – and I have dreamt of you, with all
Your sweet advantages. A mother mild
And coddling. True, she is a whore, but so's
Ophelia, that's nothing new. She loves
And, what is more, she needs you. If I were you,
I would simply poison Claudius.
Then all is square, and you can your coitus
Take with a bare whatever. I jest, Milord,
And do exceed my limit – or yours, at least.
You grimace. Think: if life's a dream, our wishes
Matter. Conform yourself to what may be
And leave the rest to molder here with me.

Juliet, Voice Over

for Sir Kenneth

No, sweetheart, it was not the lark, it's still too dark
For larks. So turn over, let me feel those bones
There in their casings, good strong bones, I love them
All. But do they all love me? This fibula,
For instance? You see: I know a word of Latin –
And you thought me dumb. Didn't you? Or ditzy.
Au contraire, mon cher. Au contraire. I know you
As though I were a hole in your head, as though . . .
Oh I don't know, it all gets too much like
A grammar lesson. Nurse? Nurse, let's play chess.
No? Yes, but history is next, and history
Is worse. History's a curse! Romeo,
Romeo, *t'amo*, but I do keep wondering
If you're not somehow a metaphor
Or metronome or metatarsal or . . . But now you think
I'm being silly and you and your dead friend
Were both so serious, I know. No, what I mean is this
(Give me a kiss): I love you, but I am
Willy-nilly a Capulet. My whims
Cost money. We can't skip off to Mantua
As though we were tinkers – now can we?
We owe the very beauty we were so skilled
To perceive in each other the decorum
Of trying to make Daddy *see*. Don't you agree?
My grammar's falling to pieces, but I love you
And I think you love me. So why don't we do
Whatever this sensible friar tells us to?

Gilda: An Entr'acte

Women are not furniture, nor yet are we angels.
So much for the Duke's and my father's arias.
As for that dear name I did go on about, I was misled
And now retract every embellishment of that song.
What is left me but to bemoan my abandonment
And view from a safe distance the dominoes
Of wickedness as they continue tumbling
Toward a logical conclusion. Oh, to be a man
And able to interpose myself between necessity
And mere, dear wish. But what have I to wish for now?
This world's an emptiness – a stage, if you like,
But the stage I'm stuck on. I must be Gilda;
I must be killed by the single person in the world
I most love. And so must you, caro nome, so must you.
Not this evening, not in the same theater, nor
To the same applause, but some day,
When the headlines require it, another body
Will be found floating in the river, another
Capo di tutti capi, and he'll be you. Alas!

Buying a Used Car

My idmost wish is not to live
Life is very often nice
But leads to grief   Let me be brief
        I want to die

But not this minute   Now I'll eat
Or watch TV or read a book
Until my brain has fogged and then
        I'll want to die

Or sleep which is as Hamlet notes
Akin to death   A test drive for
Those who aren't entirely sure
        They want to die

The salesman's suave   The price is low
It corners like a dream
You get to feel if you let go
        The thing would fly

But then you look beneath the hood
The engine is a piece of shit
Snap out of it you tell yourself
        And say good-bye

Medusa at Her Vanity

Her hair, not having breakfasted,
Coils restlessly, like anxious thoughts.
She daubs some blood into her cheeks
And smears her lips with gore.
Deaths flutter round her and alight,
Crisping their wings on her despair.

The night drags on. She tries to read.
She feeds the snakes. She yawns
Over an abyss. It's such a bore –
The books, the snakes – and it will be
Like this forever, or until the dreamt-of day
A mirror appears, to die upon her kiss.

A Gravedigger's Soliloquy

So far from denying it, we would run down
The hill pell-mell, arms windmilling like mad,
Whooping at the first glimpse of his scythe
On the horizon: 'Death! Death, we're over here!'
Until one of us would lose his breath and have to rest
On a marker, and Death would disappear
Behind a clump of shrubbery, out of sight
But still effulgent, like the moon behind a cloud.
We were as proud of our Work in that cemetery
As if we'd been hitmen for John Gotti
Or Jessye Norman's milliners, workmen at one remove
From the time's most resonant headlines.

What's supposed to come next? Anger, but who can be
Angry at easeful Death? With the Helmsleys
Perhaps, with televangelists, but not with him,
Not if one is any kind of democrat. For it is Death
Who turns history's prose to poetry,
Shaping the individual life-lines at precisely
The right unlikely moment: seeing to it
That rock stars twinkle out of existence
Before their songs have faded from the charts;
Letting the infamous shrivel, unplucked,
Until their slack and senile faces map
The warp of their souls; uprooting the infant
From its crib with the ruthless panache
Of that great American pediatrician,
William Carlos Williams, M.D., who knew
That sometimes it is enough to specify
The color of an object and the poem is there.
The color, for instance, of this gladiolus.

Take umbrage with Death? Bargain with him, rather.
There Kübler-Ross hits the nail on the head, for Death
Is not unlike a merchant of fine carpets, happy
To bicker for hours over cups of sugar-saturated tea.
He is that Isuzu salesman on TV
Whose lies we believe though we know he's lying.
Our houses fill with the junk he sells us,
Like the harbors of delta cities filling with silt,
Like our own clogged arteries and constipated bowels,
For which Death has an infallible remedy
At a price anyone can afford.

Accept his offer, therefore, in the limited time
It's available. Come live with us among the flowers
His employees have strewn upon these stately lawns.
Learn from the timeless designs of Georgia O'Keeffe
The likeness of petal and skull, of stamen
And metatarsal. Lie down beside Ophelia
In the rushing brook. Allow the gnashing
Of your teeth and his, lipless, tongueless, but
Not yet incommunicado. Accept the kiss of Death.

The Varieties of Oneiric Experience

Some dreams have big budgets from which one wakes
Grateful simply for having had so lavish a producer,
But if vast sets and gaudy special effects come to be
Taken for granted, if our inner eyes become too sophisticated,
Then increasingly we come to demand de Mille-scaled
Extravaganzas. We sate ourselves on Apocalypse Now
And cease to attend our friendly neighborhood revival
Theaters or tune in to old classics on TV. Yet these
Are often the most consoling, true three-handkerchief affairs,
Starring Garbo as Elizabeth Schwarzkopf, who is a spy
For the Resistance and not as wicked as we once believed.
Even in the roachy Thalia, even in black-and-white
That's irresistible.

                    Porn is something else again,
Whether soft or hard. While much of it may be subsumed
Under the broader category of Wish Fulfillment,
Some things happen in dreams as in life that no one in his right
        mind
Or in bright daylight would *wish* for, unless to dread
And to wish are considered synonymous. No need,
Therefore, to feel stricken about one's misdeeds in the twilight
Zone. On the other hand, we should not reject out of hand
The suggestion that there may be symbolic gold buried in the sand
Of certain idiotically reoccurring words and images.
Such dreams may be trying to tell us something but just can't
Penetrate the thick skin of the so-called 'conscious' mind:
They are like so many dimly-apprehended hands
Knocking on doors all along a long corridor at the end
Of which another, distincter hand is beckoning. Esthetically
This is cheap surrealism, and such dreams may reasonably
Be dealt with as hasty tourists deal with the long
Corridor between the Uffizi and Pitti palaces,
Which is filled from one end to the other with the portraits

And self-portraits of hundreds of artists one hasn't heard of –
That is, with a flickering, careless attention
And without slowing down.

                        The best dreams are sent
To the poor in spirit, as the Bible promises. With them
The old archetypes are still on friendly terms. For them
Babies can pop out of ovens to announce their births
And Tom and Jerry are still as funny as ever
In the eternal April of their guilelessness.
The rich man aboard his yacht, the priest at Mass beneath
Bernini's balaquin, the temptress asleep
On the speeding Orient Express: none of these know
Such sweetness, such wonder, such loving endorsements
From the Hand of the divine writer who scripts our dreams.

The Rapture

Suddenly it is all clear
I am this naked body here
Hung like a bulb upon the tree
Of Earth's exploded history

My flesh as from a sauna glows
And see how my erection grows
The world's become a single flame
And I am naked without shame

It is salvation to be lost
In such a happy holocaust
Embraced by the apocalypse
Of flesh and fire come to grips

Bomb Rome and ravish South St. Paul
Make every damned Episcopal
Pay for all the days he's seized
Burn like the sun and be well pleased

From every living cell release
Its prisoners to cloudy peace
Redeem destroy and fill with joy
All Africa and Illinois

Lift us higher make us see
The vistas of Eternity
How the godless squirm in hell
Their meat napalmed into a gel

How the blessed are whirled and tossed
Broiled by flames of Pentecost
And how at last I'm made to feel
That these bones live and I am real

Ode to Equanimity

Juno, Queen of Olympus, mighty Matriarch
Of the amortal gods, awaken again in my Mind
The infantine charm and prattle of your Gift
To those who worship Thee – myself included –
The sense of Equanimity. Goddess of the Hearth,
Send down Thy pastel Iris to shed her ever-freshening
Influence upon the Peaks and Valleys of my Moods,
Endowing them with silent Thoughts and Meditations,
Such as, in old Boeotia, the tireless Shepherds knew.
Make me as them; adjust the flow of Consciousness
To simulate the quiet purlings of the Lethe.
                    Dear Goddess, hear my Prayer!

I feel a pious Calm descend, and see
All round the gath'ring Mists of Equanimity,
As when, at dinnertime, a Colander
Of Vegetables steams in the Sink, tender to the Fork
And full of Vitamins more than sufficient to
Our daily Need. Welcome, serene Spirit,
To this Living Room! All in this home is yours,
Sweet Equanimity: the books at rest on their stained shelves,
The pans that hang upon the walls, the very paintings
In their incessant Craving to be seen –
All these belong as much to you as me.
The Music on the Phonograph, the Wine, the Cheese;
The knitted Fabrics, Cottons, Wools and silken
Polyesters that murmur soothingly of Sleep
And Dreams your sponsoring Goddess sends –
Divine Olympia, the ox-irised One, who, in the brightest Hour
Of the Noon still seems asleep, still yields the Benison
Of you, fair Equanimity!

                    But what is this!
The Telephone? No, worse, the Door! And who

Has come? Not grim Anxiety with tales of Contracts
Broken, Chances lost, of Illness and Night-Sweats?
No, not him, but Someone worse! It's drab
Half-hearted Resignation and her Spouse through all these years,
Nagging Failure. Hence, hence away, the two of you!
Here we will not think of all your serious
Concerns. I'll have the Doorman tell you I'm not home.
It's told: I am again alone with you,
My darling, Equanimity. Now nothing can disturb
Our mutual Repose. Your Lips are as the Rose
That blooms in a suburban Garden, witnessed each Day
By those who chance to pass that Way; your Eyes
Are open, but they only see your Self,
   Dear even-tempered Equanimity!

The Last Time I Saw Paris

Will I never see Paris again? It may well be.
Or Salina Cruz? Almost certainly.
But London: surely I'll live that long.
And Ischia, Naples, Capri – I must see them again,
      Although I don't know when.
      Not tomorrow, but soon.

And which are the dishes I have unwittingly
Tasted a final time? Stewed tripe? I can live
With that. Various fruits peculiar to Brazil.
But not, I beg of fate, Aunt Cece's lemon pudding.
      For I mean to make some more.
      Not tomorrow, but soon.

And which are the friends I'll see no more,
Whether by their demise or mine,
Or merely through the slow attrition
Of concern: what are their names?
      If I knew, I'd phone.
      Not tomorrow, but soon.

III

Ars Gratia Artis

Villanelle for Charles Olson

I knew him. I loved him. I sat at his feet.
Now there's a bio that says that he was
A liar, a drunkard, a leech, and a cheat,

But I still remember the way, when we'd meet,
I'd break out a joint and we'd both get a buzz.
I knew him; I loved him; I sat at his feet

While he chanted his measures of variable beat,
In the days when my mustache was nothing but fuzz.
A liar, a drunkard, a leech, and a cheat

Can still be a genius whose work can compete
With Homer's and Dante's – as *Maximus* does!
I know him. I love him. I would sit at his feet

In the kennels of hell like the dog that I was,
But now *I'm* the professor, and that is because
I knew him and loved him and sat at the feet
Of a liar, a drunkard, a leech, and a cheat.

The Book in Your Hand

It was a memorable sunset,
and the elderly poets who wrote these poems
that I have tried to read tonight
must have had their moments too.

Where the brightest orange rammed up against
the intensest blue was as satisfying as an apple,
but even better was the way their finite rows
diminished as they neared the horizon.

So on our shelves, as on the shelves we see
in photoes of forgotten writers, the titles
disappear into a solemn smudgy multitude
of bookishness, a smog of letters

all the lovelier for being indistinct.
Now this page blurs as your mind wanders
towards its own concerns. Only the sunsets
are interesting, not the effort of getting there.

'Ritin'

A Manifesto

I figure 'ritin's like workin' a lathe
More than like bobbins a-spinnin' out lace.
I figure 'ritin's a kind of a knack:
If ya got it, ya got it, if ya don't yer a hack.

Now I am not braggin', jest speakin' out plain,
But most of the 'ritin' I see is insane.
The prose is all 'ritten for someone age five,
And the poetry, dammit, there's none that's alive.

Now when I was a lad of some twelve or thirteen,
There was smut, sure enough, but it wasn't obscene.
There was books that didn't jest try an' unnerve us,
And the best of those books was by Robert Service.

Oh, he did us a service, all right, did ol' Bob!
Cuz he wasn't a pansy an' wasn't a snob,
Jest a plain-spoken fella with a workin' man's way
Of sayin' what he had in him to say.

He talked about wimen, he talked about booze,
But he sure didn't talk like the Nine O'Clock News.
He could preach, God bless him, and preach like a pro,
But what he did best was, he understood snow.

Now yer snow is a killer, and so are some men,
An ol' Bobby Service, why, he knew 'em when.
He knew 'em in New York, he knew 'em in Nome,
And he stuck every one of 'em into a poem!

An Bob did it, I'll betcha, by seem' things square,
Then settin em down with not one word to spare,

Like a good line of rivets, or a tol'rance so true
You knew that his stories could happen to you.

So that's why I say of all writers there are,
The best of the lot was Bob Service by far,
And all of you eggheads up there on Parnassus,
Should do jest like he did and get up off yer asses.

Womankind and Poesy

a Parable

'Because formal poetry has
an obvious place in the male
tradition, many contemporary
feminist poets have rejected it
completely, accused women of
working in those traditions of
buying into the patriarchy'
FROM A REVIEW IN *Open Places*

Cassandra stood outside the gate
Scarce able to express her hate
For traitors to their sex whose verse
Would rhyme or scan. On them her curse:
Should any woman ever write
As patriarchal acolyte
Let her sisters ever treat her
Strictly as her strictest meter,
Binding tight her tender feet
And beating her when she would cheat
By throwing in an anapest.
Then round about her swelling chest
Let constraining couplets wind
Till she cry out to Womankind:

O my dear sisters
forgive me if you can
I have been writing like a
        patriarch
    but now I've seen the error
    of my ways
            and by Gaea
                    I'm free!

Colloquy

Would you write and be respected –
    Reviewed, remaindered, paperbacked,
Sales in millions, poems collected?
    Yes I would, as a matter of fact.
Then tow the line, do what's expected,
    And let your middle name be Tact.

Deplore such follies of the age
    As waste and crime and air pollution,
But never in the tones of rage.
    With, you mean, circumlocution?
Well, not exactly that: be sage,
    And try to make a contribution.

Yet in deploring do not fail
    To credit those who've gone before you.
Even if they've gone to jail?
    I see that I begin to bore you.
Excuse me: what I meant was 'Yale.'
    Sneer, and I shall just ignore you,

And so, dear boy, will tout le monde.
    Have a regard for privilege,
And leave your razor wit unhoned:
    Dullness gives a better edge.
So kind of you to telephone,
    And thank you for the tutelage,

But really, Dean, it's not my style
    To back out when I can affront,
Or mask my rancor with a smile.
    It is my nature to be blunt.
And mine to be a crocodile?
    No, I would say a cunt.

Gods

If they are not to be
    Pure geometry,
Gods should wear no clothes,
    And those who do,
Like this bronze Mars
    In Monument Park,
Cuirassed and helmeted,
    Invite suspicion
As to their divinity.
    (His pedestal
Allegorizes him as merely
    Military Courage.)
One dry fountain
    And two lawns away
An older eidolon expresses
    The same idea
More forcefully: a bronze
    Lion by Bayre.
There beyond his leonine
    Majesty, a living god
In a flesh-colored loincloth
    Slathers himself
With tanning lotion.
    Now he sprawls
His splendors on the grass.
    What majesty,
And what an ass!

The Cubist Paintings of Lesser Museums

Alas, they have grown so old!
It seems only yesterday
I was a teenager myself, cheering
For the demolition of the bourgeoisie
(It's easier to dislike people in French,
Isn't it?) – and now, voici,
C'est moi, en musée, voyant
Les cubistes anciens, and mon dieu,
How weathered, how faded, how very often
Simply inane. Even Juan Gris
Has days when when he ought not have
Bothered coming to the office.

There are, this would suggest,
No dependable answers. Either
You bring it off or you don't.
Here is the same mind, the same
Reciprocating engine of hand and eye,
But something has gone wrong. Why?

How old, how faded.
Tomorrow, one wishes to whisper
To such paintings, tomorrow
You will be bright again.

At the Van Gogh Museum

The lesson here? It's very clear: we can
By making friends with you endure the whole
Mad scramble of life, the shoving and the shoveling,
Knowing through this friendship that every year
Will yield its blossoms and its beards, its spears
Of jade green thrusting from gnarled brown bulbs,
Its saturations of humanity's and flowers'
Insistence on being *seen*, an insistence we must learn
After a time to put by, dropping the blossoms,
Cropping off an ear, because you, after all,
Are near – as a wind, a whisper, a glint in the eye
Of Baby Camille Roulin. Unhappiness
Is sure, but surer perhaps for the poor
Living far from the decorous interiors of Paris,
Their pain unrecognized as such, blessed
Only by their nearer proximity to you, who are
The last divinity left: Death. Dark blue Death
Stark behind the scumblings of the clouds,
Implicit in all greens, mocker of all *machers*,
Confounder of lust. All the golds of rich September
Turn to khaki at your touch, and lamplight
Is a feeble contradiction, books a fiction,
Flesh a fable that can only be recalled
In a dead Christ after Delacroix, in Rembrandt's
Livid and unrisen Lazarus. The brushstrokes
Layer brushstrokes like an infinite regression
Of quotation marks telling us what men
Were once reported to believe. Just so,
In the Nieuwe Kerk our art historians
Discover crude gothic angels beneath the reforming
Whitewash of the Protestants; just so, when Vincent
Wiped away each canvas's white lie,

He found the sooty windows of his youth, the same
Warped faces and lightless spaces that first
Acquainted him with you – prussian blue,
Phthalocyanine, cerulean Death!

Fashion Statements

The man who wears plaid is a man willing
                              to face contradictions.
Harris tweed bespeaks another, though no
                              less commendable mentality.
Eccentricity and evident expense are
                              equally to be deplored.

Modesty must needs be an unconscious grace, not to be
Achieved by dint of chinos and reticent neckware.
Nuns in old movies always look false; likewise, trustfunders
                              dressed up as lumberjacks.

With shoes utility is all that matters. The greatest
                              fashion revolution of the 80s
Has been the freedom to wear sneakers to the office.
Only be ostentatious where ostentation's *comme il faut*.

White is for summer and then primarily
                              as a declaration of innocence.
Elastic, however it functions, should be concealed.
An anxious amalgam of colors is all right,
                              if *you* are anxious.
Routinely dispose of stained ties and threadbare socks.
Suspenders are better than belts for the very obese.

Place your trust in the advice of a responsible salesperson.
Loosen the knot of your tie when you wish to suggest
An accord has been reached; remove it,
If it appears that first estimate was mistaken.
Don't wear a baseball cap unless you have
                              strong opinions about baseball.

In Rome, dress to the hilt; in Paris, dress to kill.
Soft fabrics loosely draped ask to be touched.

At least once a week use a good deodorant.

Machismo needs to be set off with a sprig of femininity,
As when a pair of shitkicker boots has floral insets.
Never, however, think you can get away with a kilt.

Wear pajamas to bed when staying the night with friends.
Iron even those shirts that don't strictly require it.
Let your beard get bushy once every few years.
Launder handkerchiefs in the sink with a little Woolite,
                       not with the rest of the wash.
Inkstains on shirtpockets can usually be construed as
Nonchalance or a wholesome parsimony, like
                       visible mends and darns.
Good taste is what one's tribe decrees. Love your totems
                       and you'll always look well.

Toupees are as basic a don't as elevator shoes.
Own up to the hand heredity's dealt you, and compensate
                       with loud ties and garish shirts.

Follow fashion as you vote for a president, trusting that,
Among limited options, your choice is the likeliest to last
                       four years, with luck even eight.
Character is expressed in the flexibility with which
                       one moves between
Extremes of playfulness and sobriety, blue suede and blue
                       serge, bunnyrabbit and grizzly.

Consider the business suit, how it flatters no figure,
Offers no advantage except that of anonymity, equates
                       banker and gangster, the same in
New York as in Dallas, in Tokyo as in Turin.
Tacit in its tailoring is a respect for medians and
                       the law of averages.
Ribbons and braid, which feature so prominently
                       in the semiologies of *Gloire*,

Are antithetical to the three-piece suit, whose *raison*
D'être, since it first evolved in tandem with
                                        the triple-decker novel,
Is the decision to let the other sex assume the onus of
Conspicuous consumption, of responding to annual variations
                                        in hemlines and fall colors.
The charm of Cary Grant, the wonder of Fred Astaire,
                                        their durability as
Icons of popular culture, derives in good part from
                                        the way they made the uniform
Of an officially classless society seem to have class.
Not what they wore made their names synonyms for
Style, but the expressive motions of the beast within.

Quilt

In the arts of Islam   Pattern takes control   Images being forbidden
Images being forbidden   In the arts of Islam   Pattern takes control
Pattern takes control   Images being forbidden   In the arts of Islam

Images being forbidden   In the arts of Islam   Pattern takes control
In the arts of Islam   Pattern takes control   Images being forbidden
Pattern takes control   Images being forbidden   In the arts of Islam

Pattern takes control   Images being forbidden   In the arts of Islam
In the arts of Islam   Pattern takes control   Images being forbidden
Images being forbidden   In the arts of Islam   Pattern takes control

In the arts of Islam   Pattern takes control   Images being forbidden
Images being forbidden   In the arts of Islam   Pattern takes control
Pattern takes control   Images being forbidden   In the arts of Islam

Images being forbidden   In the arts of Islam   Pattern takes control
In the arts of Islam   Pattern takes control   Images being forbidden
Pattern takes control   Images being forbidden   In the arts of Islam

Pattern takes control   Images being forbidden   In the arts of Islam
In the arts of Islam   Pattern takes control   Images being forbidden
Images being forbidden   In the arts of Islam   Pattern takes control

Inventory

Crammed ever tighter, stacked ever higher,
     all jammed together, the artifacts
Of fifty years agglomerate in cupboards,
     closets, cartons, drawers and shelves
Until one final fatal freebie triggers
     the avalanche and the levee fails,
The seeds split their pods, the spores
     disperse to mushroom eveywhere:
Heaps of cast-off clothing climb the backs
     of chairs, then shoot out threads
That cling to moldings and lamp poles
     which soon are festooned with webs
Of underwear and overalls; stacks of paperbacks
     ascend on both sides of the toasters
And form a bridge to the ziggurat of stereo
     components where a horde of extras –
White elephants, senile Walkmen, silly
     69¢ tshotchkes, unsprung windups –
Re-enact Griffith's *Intolerance*; the magazines
     become a liquid mass that breaks
Against the pilings of the coffee table; the air
     rustles with bills paid to vanished
Department stores, still shimmering like willow
     leaves, still insistent as tombstones
On the facts they commemorate, purchases
     and purposes else lost to history;
Dishes spill from their secret places, flotsam
     on the tide of periodicals, awash
In the wrack of a lifetime's robinsonade:
     cans of dry putty, coils
Of clothesline, nests of flowerpots, plastic
     jack-o'-lanterns and Easter baskets,
And the gleanings of a dozen shingled beaches –
     things of beauty, toys forever,

To release one's grip on any of which
        would be to accede to Heracleitus
That nature's a promiscuous flame, one wick
        the same to it as another,
No single seashell lovelier than the rest,
        all estimations of worth
As arbitary as the prices van Gogh got
        in his lifetime or gets now in Japan;
Now's the time to call the Savonarola
        Extermination Service, but no, too late,
Already that memo is a fossil in the rich
        deposits of the desk, lost among pencils
And lapsed warrenties; already the third telephone,
        ringing with terror, has crawled beneath
The bed to enlist in its limbo of dustballs
        and old shoes, some scarcely worn,
While within the tiered suitcases atop the closet
        rumors of annihilation spread:
Trousers that have waited years for waists
        to match their waistlines, tee-shirts
That have told the same joke too many times,
        bold prints that want their former
Confidence – all foresee the bonfires
        of their vanity; so must a foetus
Feel at the first whisper of the word Abort
        or dinosaurs as the comet appears
Announcing their extinction, inexorable
        and all unmerited; – or as the texts
That Heracleitus in his heyday wrote
        and thought immortal, which were
Preserved in Alexandria's great library
        a little while and then incinerated.

A Galop for Cesar Franck

I

Who is, mon cher chasseur maudit,
    The biggest shark in all the sea?
The carnivore to end all carnivores?
    I know it isn't me.

Although I feel I must be near
    The end of the food chain.
You see my net? You see my spear?
    Be careful: I'm insane.

I hear you stir, I leap aside.
    You lunge; I feint; you cry!
You come for me, but I've denied
    Your god and you must die.

2

    Our conductors
look, for the most part, like businessmen,
    and, like businessmen
they can unleash titanic forces.

    I am not musical –
can only dance, i.e., pretend to be
    propelled by the beat,
and that not well. But then George Szell

    is not himself
titanic. There is a force beneath
    the music we understand,
and composers themselves, those supreme

human beings,
were, like the rest of us, the servants
of its commands.
Hear it! whirling through the world,

exultant; damned.

Symphonic Ode for St. Cecilia's Day

for Greg Sandow

I PERCUSSION

Boom thump crash:
Like a haunted cow
Climbing the stairs
Of a rented cottage,

The timpani's
Thunders explain
To the complaining heart
How, most energetically, to beat.

Like this, like this –
Not, as you have beat so long,
Unthinkingly, but like this.
The heart murmurs an apology.

Too late. Something
Has sentenced us to death.
We will listen forever
To fantastic symphonies.

Forever: imagine
How long that must be!
There we'll be, eternally,
Flitting about heaven,

Dipping, soaring, strumming
Our golden harps, clapping
For the archangels,
And having as much fun

As a pair of disembodied hands
Possibly can. One understands,
Fleetingly, why the man who invented dynamite
Also gave his name to peace.

But what is it one has just understood?
Already one has forgotten
Everything but the amazement
Of having felt so good.

2   WOODWINDS

The clarinet is in its nest
Hatching baby clarinets
And feeding them worms.
The sun is warm as butter

As it melts on toast
And you fall in love.
Woodwinds are always falling in love
And being abandoned.

'Plangent' is the apposite marking.
Maybe the reason lies in the reed itself,
As it disintegrates under the gale
Force of the melody.

'But maybe all melodies are beyond
Explanation,' the flutes, abetted
By the piccolos suggest. 'Are snowflakes
Knowable, for all their symmetries?

Who has not sometime stood
Bewildered by the colors
Of Monet's peaches and grapes?'
'Not I,' replies a man in gray.

'I am no popinjay esthete, I.
I have never read Wallace Stevens.
I have invested my money wisely.
I will never die,

And when I do, shepherds shall place
Rue and myrtle on my grave.
Then shall ponderous bassoons arise
From the braches of willows and cypresses

To fill the blue and violet sky
With manic ideas and delightful noise.'
Thus spake the man in the gray suit
Before a painting of a bowl of fruit.

3 BRASSES

The trumpet's bright clamor
Incites us to murder.
Join *our* brigade, they jubilate,
Filling our glasses with free wine.

They're crazy, those trumpets,
But one understands their appeal.
Blowing up bridges, sexy uniforms,
Rage without guilt. Why not?

The horns know why. Life can be agreeable
Without risk or exertion.
One only need forget
That evil exists. Listen:

Across the lake!
The sound of the moon,
The lapping of waves, the movement
Of large animals through the trees.

Yes, but there are many instincts,
And each must be followed where it leads.
I am only one trombone,
But when there are five other trombones with me

Nothing could be louder
Or better declare the primacy of instinct,
The utter joy of being a trombone,
Of being six trombones, all playing together!

That is not a possibility, however,
Open to everyone. To a tuba, for instance.
Some of us have families.
Some of us have jobs.

I believe that teamwork is required.
I do what I'm told.
Sometimes though, sometimes I dream
I'm a trumpet, and it makes me smile.

4 STRINGS

Continuous movement without breath;
Love, therefore, in some other sense
Than rapture. In the sense, perhaps,
That the helices of deoxyribonucleic acid

May be said to love
The wand they're wound around.
You know, do you not, that the wires
Of lyres and all things stringed,

When they are plucked or bowed,
Form double curves along the axis
Defined by the strings drawn taut?
A caduceus, as it were,

Or – a molecule of DNA.
The violin itself's
A Cubist rendering
Of the strings' complex vibrations –

An artisan's homage
To the inexplicable
Completeness and tidiness
Of the universe,

To the music, *comme on dit,*
Of the spheres,
Which is a music, admittedly,
No one actually hears (and so

All the sweeter, maybe, for that,
If we're to believe Keats).
Yes, if music's any indication,
Our universe is neat as a pin.

Yet does it finally make any sense?
Does the hand that follows these windings
Into the heart of the mind
Ever touch anything solidly there?

IV

Theories of Other People

The Crumbling Infrastructure

A limb snaps, the hive is smashed, and the survivors
Buzz off to colonize another neck of the woods.
No nest is sacrosanct. Abandoned churches may serve
A while as discotheques. Steel towns may hope
To be retooled to meet the needs of foreign banks
Anxious to reinvest evaporating capital
Beyond the reach of ruin. But generally decay's
The aftermath of desuetude. Rome,
What's left of it, falls to the Hun, and all
Its noble plumbing is undone. The fountains
Of Versailles run dry, and the Bourbons are remembered
As a lower-class alternative to Scotch.
In all these matters money rules, but not as the sun,
Benign, inscrutable, and far away, but as a river would,
Collating the waters of a hundred townships,
Tolerant of dams, a source of wonder and a force
Even the Federal Reserve cannot coerce.
Basements flood, canoeists (i.e., small investors)
Drown, and nothing can be done about the mosquitoes,
But on the whole one does well to dwell in the valley.
Money, like water, yields an interest hard to deny.
Every dawn brings new quotations in the pages
Of The Times; every sunset gilds the thought of death
As though it were the mummy of a king.
Then is every man an Emerson,
Aghast at the everlasting, wild with surmise,
His daily paper dewy with the news
Of history's long, slow slouch toward
That Götterdammerung dearest to pulp
Illustrators: Liberty's torch thrust up,
Excalibur-like, from the sands of a new Sahara
Or the waves of a new flood, her bronze flame
All that remains of Babylon. A pretty sight –

But meanwhile Liberty's toes are dry, bridges
And tunnels still traversable, and someone had better
Be paid to patch these goddamn potholes, that's all
I'm trying to say, because if they're not,
Someone's going to break an axle, and it could be one of us.

Class Notes

Rocky Mountain Ramble

The poor, if they are self-possessed, may share
These views, provided the self they possess
Is reasonably becoming. Read Hemingway
To see how it's done. He was the paid companion
Par excellence. In his democracy of skiers
And good shots, where a simple guide may be
Manlier than many millionaires, arête
Is the password. Wit is not called for here,
And those who live by it, in an atmosphere
Of crystal, silver and swift reparte', would here
Be out of place. Here language is 'honed down'
To the basic palaver of Greystoke,
Whom even apes may apprehend and must obey.
No wonder Papa's books are assigned to all classes.
Practice such protocols and *you* may learn
To be a ski instructor too, exalted to a like degree,
Sharing the platonic form of Millionaire.
But be aware there is a price to pay, not just
Wit's richer vocabulary and its license to be snide
About *jeunesse dorée,* but the obligation to risk
One's life on a regular basis, to taste the self-
Apotheosizing *vin extraordinaire* of mortal danger.
Drunk on such brew, laurels seem spontaneously
To wreathe one's brow. What did Dryden say? None
But the brave, none but the brave, deserve the fair.
And what better proof of bravery than to have returned
Alive from the perilous jeep-ride or the theater of war?
O to have skied the Plunge and have the fact
Be known to one's beholders! It is a wine
Past all compare. Drinking it, one *must* believe
In the divine right of kings. We are then kings
Ourselves, and heirs of empires.

2

So much for the brave: what of the fair?
What of August's meadows at the top
Of the trail? What of these butterflies? What of
These many-aspened galleries of timeless art,
The true Conceptualism of the rampant eye
Snapping Monet after Monet in the stillness
Of these higher altitudes, above the crags
Where eagles dare — though, really, where's the daring
Of it for an eagle? They must feel quite at home
Up here. See how they ride the breezes langorous
As Cleopatra on her barge. Rarely is there need
To rapture prey, and the hours would pass away
Almost wholly in contemplation, were it not
For the flies and the sudden discovery amid
These pastoral vistas of a mining camp,
Abandoned, slowly turning into scree.
Here men enjoyed the mountain air who were
Neither kings nor Hemingways. Do they weep
There where they've gone to their reward
To see their tenements so forgotten and forlorn?
Would any modern Goldsmith mourn
Their loss? Goldsmith — the very word
Is like a bell to toll me back to my hotel
In the valley far below, to all the comforts
And confusions, the names and dates, the daily news
And unpaid dues, and terms of sufferance,
Thence to the city we have named our home,
Inapprehensible Reality.

Death Wish IV

The well-meaning young of South Africa,
The decent whites we could imagine talking to,
Are committing suicide in record numbers
As they are conscripted for military duty
And find themselves unequal to the task
Of murder. The statistics are in *The Times*.

But isn't it so that we all commit crimes?
The very blacks protesting this state of affairs
Some of them anyhow, are using crack to crank
Will to where it will perform like Robin Hood,
Fantomas, whoever's the latest king of scuzz,
And if he isn't a hero to you or me, that's only because

We're cowards and so craven we'll admit it
The moment the FBI asks. This is the end of the world,
We all know that, and no one so incautious
As to be reading this would ever deny Proposition One:
That we are resolved to pursue our advantages
Into the very tarpits of extinction. We will die

As stoutly as the dimmest dinosaurs, but we
Will take the world with us, this time, state by state,
Niche by niche, each of us applauding the exit
Of our predecessor. Tonight it was Lerner,
Borges, Benny Goodman. Tomorrow? Exponentially
More. How boring even the headlines are. How I lust

For more: I want all Antarctica to calve
Its mountains into the sea, I want to see vast
Shores erased, and read effusive epitaphs
For my imaginary enemies. I want all human flesh
To wear its death upon its sleeve. I want
To curse my birth, and drown in drink, and grieve.

Nether: a Traveler's Notes

We go there when we want to be alone
For an indefinite period, checking in
Under an alias we of course forget
At the first real identity crisis.
We take in all the sights in one weekend
And then there's nothing left but the strange cuisine,
The daily mudbath in the hotel's spa,
And expeditions to the Grand Bazaar
With all its inexplicable handicrafts.
Life can be lived in such different ways:
That is the secret wisdom of the tourist.
The residents know secrets deeper still,
A knowledge that invests their smiles
With the proverbial charm of Nether.
Two weeks there and we begin to be
Insatiable for any evidences of
Our own folkways – clocks divided
In units of sixty, women with both arms and legs,
Domestic animals with their natural names;
Above all, ice cream made as we remember it
With pieces of our own internal economy
Smooshed in. The craving grows for all
That can be known without examination,
For the drab, assuring twilights of home.
But still we linger there, professional students
Doomed ever to audit the universe's
University, proud that we may never
Attain a degree and thereby stop
Inquiring of the statue here in the temple
Said to have been devoted anciently
To Isis (although our guidebook
Expresses some skepticism about that),
Inquiring of her how to reconcile
Our sense of freedom with the fluxions of the Nile.

A Stroll Through Moscow

One expects it to be dull, and is not disappointed.
Many of the usual pedestrian pleasures
Are absent here, and not having done my homework
In this odd alphabet, I'm at a loss to interpret
Even the few shopfronts that exist. This one, for instance:
What does it sell? Shoes? Newspapers? The cues

Are minimal. But I'm not here to indite one more *J'accuse!*
Only to spend some time and rubles. I ask no pointed
Questions and try to adopt the ingenuous stance
Of a tourist, which, after all, I am. Whatever pleasures
Mere looking allows I'll have, and try not to interpret
(Till I'm home) the frowns and snubs of those whose work

Requires them to be impolite. I've had to work
At jobs almost as onerous, though I hadn't their excuse
(No ideology, that is) for rudeness. They interpret
Even my Levis as arrogance. How the spy appointed
To tail me must hate Americans: our cash, our pleasures,
The very sneakers on our feet, each an illicit substance

In his eyes, each another hateful instance
Of a world (ours) that rewards Those Who Don't Work
At the expense (his) of those who do. But pleasures
Of any sort are suspect here. 'Mind your P's and Q's,'
I was told at the embassy, when I asked to be pointed
The way to the Kremlin, advice I find hard to interpret.

Should an official 'visiting poet' have to interpret
Every paranoid enigma? Isn't a polite resistance
To unthinking hostility my first duty, my appointed
Task? Isn't it, in point of fact, the 'work'
Of a writer to do whatever's done, to join the queues
For cabbage, drink kvass, and share such pleasures

As are commonly available? I could wish those pleasures
Larger and more various – but I refuse to interpret
The present paucity, the scowls, the ubiquitous queues
As a sign that Russia's somehow doomed to its stance
Of intransigent *ressentiment*. The future didn't work,
But another future can. So, am I *totally* disappointed?

No. But I wouldn't want to be appointed attaché. Pleasure's
Too much work here, and pain's its pay. I can't interpret,
In these circumstances, war and peace and queues.

Haikus of an AmPart

Bombay luggage rats
Scrabble for my Samsonite
I inhale the stench

Everyone loves you
All the market's food is free
Here in Cow Heaven

Gutter water goes
Into a big bronze ewer
For dinner tonight

Dinner at the Taj
A goat killed at Kali's shrine
@ 200 rupees

Three extra crosswords –
All the luggage must be screened
After the bomb threat

But for the songbirds
The cathedral is empty
God needs no people

No one knew its name
Till Rangarajan told me –
A jacaranda!

Grandma Gilbertson
Would have loved this doctor's kitsch
And his wife's cooking

Shyly he tells me
I look like Geoffrey Chaucer
He? Siva, surely

At eight bucks a beer
The Sheraton has made me
A teetotaler

Their best crimes dwarf ours
One man had both legs cut off
On a busy street

How quickly dishes
Disappear, how slow the check –
Waiters' catlike smiles

Of Delhi I'll know
Only this parking lot view
A toilet my home

Lomotil's no help
Five days of diarrhea
What morsel did this?

Huge Sikhs man the doors
Hell has no servant problem
Nor edible trash

Waiting for takeoff
What do we hear? Not Muzak –
A Hitchcock soundtrack

Hovels from on high
Lahore from God's point of view
A shattered hive

The Consulate's duck
Waddles among the mullahs
Waiting for green cards

A helicopter
Propeller above the bed –
Rotary mantras

Islamic women
Are allowed one profession
Gynecology

Unfair to Allah
Illiterates rioting
Against written words

Eagles, more eagles
Women bundled in black rugs
Kuwait airport art

Skeletons in shrouds
Chainsmoke and scowl at all us
Materialists

Engine by New York
And body by Miami
Shalom Tel Aviv

Heaven seems closer
On Jerusalem rooftops
Fatal attraction

City without bums
Is it the chill in the air
Or the machine guns?

'Where's the Sheraton?'
In Hebrew it means toilet
'There,' people say, 'there!'

We Are Divided Everywhere in Two Parts

The subcontinent is divided in two parts,
Much like your heart or mine, one receptive
To new data, the other an armed camp, a bloody hell,
And those two parts in turn subdivided,
And so forth and so on, just as Malthus predicted,
Until some limit is reached when the halves
Become halve-nots, too desperately poor
To do anything but pantomime starvation
At the drivers of the cars brought up short before
The city's single traffic light. No one here
Has much use for laws. Anyone guilty
Of an accident is simply beaten to death
By a mob, who have left off, for a moment,
Making love to their invisible wives
Back home at the arsenal. Even to imagine
These women is accounted, by one half the subcontinent,
An offense punishable by blinding. So let us
At once banish the thought of women from our poems
And just suppose nothing's alive beneath those clothes,
The fluttering saris, the black polyester bedspreads
With only a half-inch slit to peek through. Indeed,
We can let the men achieve the same invisibility
And turn our attention from the blood-stained street
To the kites circling above, emblematic
Of our longing to return this minute to the airport
And re-enter the womb of a homebound 747, the known mix
Of nomadic monads in the sky's great cocktail
Shaker, home to lives whose structure we comprehend,
Whose smells we savor, where, with a sweet
Sigh of relief and cries of *Thou! Thou!*, we may
Repackage our selfs in the wrappers of our beloved
Consumer society, where the water is safe
And the women in their blue jeans are visible and eager
To explain that we've understood nothing

We've seen, that most people are really basically good,
A proposition to which, once home, I willingly accede,
Quite as I dye eggs at Easter and write on them
Our names and those of our imaginary friends.

Ah, but I'm not in that dichotomous There-with-You yet.
I'm still Here on the left side of the subcontinent,
Relishing its strangenesses, and you are a thought
In the other lobe of the globe, a mote in the eye
Of a different Omnipotence, a world away,
Imagining me perhaps (I like to think so)
Riding an elephant. How large we bulk
In our supposing of how we're seen: nothing less
Than a howdah will do. How *do* I do?
It's nice of you to ask, and I am in
A howdah's contemporary equivalent, and purdah, too,
For this is the day that Pakistan celebrates
Its nationhood, and I have been borne off
To a perfect replica of the dear There where you are –
Indeed, a perfecter – a 21st century howdah
Replete with Taster's Choice, Comet, and cheddar cheese.
Only the muezzin 's amplified moans mar the illusion
I'm home unestranged, and even these may be misconstrued
As failed music. Here I'm secure against
Most forms of harm too-visible Americans may be prey to.
Here the icebox is an oasis of drinkables. Here
What seems to be happening begins to make sense,
Though that is not to say I could answer the question
We aliens are forever volleying back and forth:
What does it all mean? What clue or clipping has my eye
Passed over, what peppercorn of significance,
What crystal image needing only the moisture
Of a passing ballpoint to unfurl and quadruple
Into an adequate diagram of the sentences
In this exam, ample enough to contain
All necessary qualifiers, such as 'over-eager,'
'Vain,' and 'inchoate,' without losing the velocity

Of the verbs, or nouns' pronouncements of the names
Of everyone arriving at the party a polite hour late,
Pronounced and instantly misfiled –
For what is my western Rolodex to do
With Muqbar-ibn-Wallah-Quaid-i-Azim? –
Becoming in that instant of misapprehension
Not even he or she, for Urdu has transcended
Gender, but only someone here now and gone
Tomorrow, which in Urdu is the same as yesterday,
A misfortune that the framers of the language
Could not have foreseen, any more than we of the West
Foresaw the greenhouse effect when we equipped our cinemas
And embassies with air conditioners. Wouldn't you
Rather die in a cool room among crisp-petalled flowers
Than be gunned down in the street by madmen
Who can't take the heat? These are not the only choices:
It's only the damnable (choose one) duality of those
Twins, tomorrow and yesterday, that frazzles the nerves
Of us professional fusspots and makes us unable
To welcome each dish of weird deliciousness as it appears
On the buffet table of Today. What we should do
Is declare this *our* national holiday too and don our best
Be Happy! tees and count cadence down the Fifth Avenue
Of Here and Now, a memorable yesterday east of us,
An exciting tomorrow to the west, boys and girls together.

Slouches

The cowboy's is most to be envied, a slouch
Reserved for the slim, shoulders slumping
Forward, the spine relaxing at a point midway
Between collar and belt,
                              a posture
The potbellied cannot sustain, for when *they* yield
To the tug of gravity it is primarily the paunch's
Demand that must be met,
                              the upper torso
                                        tilting
Backwards to form a beam from which the gut
Can be slung: no slouch is so tiresome, so lacking
Benefit or grace.

          Let us in charity
Avert our gaze, to contemplate the slouch
Of the effete and epicene, a limpness
Of muscular being so intrinsic, seemingly,
As not to register at once as a slouch
But simply as one of the many terms
Of an unconditional surrender:
A deceit patent as the undulations of a squid's
Suckered tentacles. Beware the spineless:
They may have beaks.

                    How sweet, by contrast,
The slouch of the couch potato taking its ease
Before the horrors of the Six O'Clock News,
Comfortable within a cocoon of cushioning
Ironies,
          certain of the meal ahead and then
Of whatever sitcom fate has ordained

Before the time for bed and the Sealy
Posturpedic's irresistible solicitation
To the slouch that even the stiffest D.I.,
Even Arnold Schwarzenegger, succumbs to
When the cards are down, the slouch of sleep.

Rules of Order for New Conservatives

Here is another chance to hear it
the voice that asks you to come
nearer & tells you to obey

I am Authority, you hear it
calling like a mullah from the
minaret of the assembled wisdom
of the commonplace

                    Should you
go near it you may find yourself
to be merely a member of the race
& necessarily replaceable

Breed & pasture as you're told
& see you get your weekly fleecing
Follow your leaders to realms of gold
Never say goddamn   Defer
So few & simple are the rules

                    I am
being serious but not sincere

for it lies within me to suppose
the lies reverberating in the mosque
may be the givens of some higher math
occluded consciousness misapprehends

that life may bend us to its ends
by mysteries embodied in the unseen
migrations in the sea
the crunching of large numbers
& an acquaintance with calligraphy

Selah

Summer of '88

We are the Pepsi Generation, no other epithet fits
    half so well, who grew up flooring the pedal

Ground our hips to the hits of the Beach Boys, dumb blonds
    who'd made the ocean their plaything

Found the secret button that told our neurons It feels so good
    let's do it again, let's wash our dishes

In Joy, smoke Trues, power our cars with a gas that expresses
    our totemic affinity with extinct species

Have another, don't mind if I do, while somewhere in Bolivia
    brain-damaged Indians labored like aphids to produce

The magic beans we larvae needed to keep the screens
    of prime time brimming with images

The fun was inescapable as sunlight and every petal
    opened to its influence, Mother Teresa

Flew to Bombay to comfort the dying with the dry caress
    of anorexic hands, Philippine fishermen

Bombed coral reefs to stun rare fish so they might die
    in our aquariums, such was our regard

For death's sacred loveliness, and if our motives
    were a riddle, tragedy does not require

The hero wittingly to invite Nemesis, it is enough
    to feel a little shiver of dread as the hum

Of the air conditioner comes on, cooling the theater
    and renovating the atmosphere, molecule by incremental

Molecule, a sense of Of course as the glamorous Sun Belt
    expands to meet popular demand until even North Dakota

Glows with groves of grapefruit and gondolas cruise
    Old Times Square, going Putt! Putt! Putt!

Emitting more of the same vapors, because you don't suppose
    do you that anything will be done

Rats given a choice between a pellet of food and a zap
    direct to the pleasure center will always choose

The zap and so die happy: crack seems to work
    the same way, and so the nuclear family fissions

To its irreducible minimum, a foetus addicted
    to the snap crackle and pop of Oh that feels good

Let's go faster, let's fly to Mars and see if the face
    in the photograph is really human or only

An accidental configuration of a lifeless desert
    would you like another, yes please that was delicious

Gays and spayed cats have it easiest, no need to fret
    for nephews and nieces, it's not our progeny

Who'll be deeded with a houseboat on Love Canal
    for us it's Malibu in the summer of '88

So come on, hop in, enjoy the planet while it spins
    the party won't be over for x-many years

Centennial Tankas

The Brooklyn Bridge is
100 years old tonight
Let's raise our glasses

And praise it as we would wish
To be praised if we'd raised it

It mirrors the size
We grew to, who went through this
Century with it

Aorta and pulsing vein
Of Success's golden heart

Prophet of profits
Grandstand of suicides, theme
Of all boozy bards

Wonder of the Average Man
Pyramids blink at its span

And churches shudder
They can see above its towers
Cities in the stars

Pervigilium Veneris 1991

Let every homeless person find a home tonight;
Let those who stay at home be snug and tight.

May empty bottles in the trash barrels fill
With every vagrant's favorite swill.

Bacchus, plumb the ribs we've gnawed
With mean as savory as we'd serve a god.

From all that's waste and without use
Extract some unsuspected juice.

Invite a joyful populace to share
Your cloud-capped refuge from despair,

And from Olympus's own Helmsley Palace
Rain down delights on every Ralph and Alice.

Array with blossoms and offer as brides
Fair nymphs to our potential suicides.

Disguise your own divinity and join
The whores and hustlers of the Tenderloin

To celebrate the abrogation of
All laws that cannot trace their source to Love.

Let every homeless person find a home tonight;
May those who stay at home be snug and tight.

To the Young Mercenaries

Soldiers of Fortune, not yet nineteen,
With steel-toed boots and cheeks daubed green,
Don't think we cannot see you through
These camo games of peekaboo.

We do. We see you, but must turn
Our cheeks that otherwise might burn
With conscious shame of having spied,
Approvingly, at homicide.

Go, dear boys, and wash your faces.
Then come back to the emptied places.
See, here's a chair, and here's another,
And here's the corpse of someone's mother.

Why, what a spacious world you've made!
Now, are you clean, and were you paid?
No, I see there still are traces
Of sin and death upon your faces.

Go, wash again, and while you do,
We'll send policemen after you.
The world you've made so spacious we
May now inhabit, peacefully.

After Péguy

Happy those heroes who die for the sexy earth,
So long as they fought in a justified war.
Happy those heroes who die a four-square death,
A death that's grave and dignified.

Happy those heroes who die on famous battlefields,
Laid out before the beaming face of God,
Heroes who die on top of high hills
With all the clutter of classy funerals.

Happy those heroes who die for the burnt cities,
For such cities are the corpse of the City of God;
Happy those who die for fireplace and fire,
Clutching a letter from the folks back home.

Because such stuff is emblematic
Of Heaven's infinite furniture.
Happy those heroes who die embarrassed
For having expired in a drunken stupor.

Because from the stupors of this world they shall pass on
To the stupors of Eternity.
Happy those heroes whom shrapnel disembowels
Even as they are blinded.

Because their honor and their poetry will linger on
As the odor of bay leaves in an empty tin
In a bombed shop in a ruined village
In the glorious charnel-house of France.

A Benevolent Demi-Villanelle

Pity the bigots who scream and yell.
They're victims of their lack of class
And cannot help the way they smell

Of cheap perfume and muscatel.
They're loud and coarse and shrill and crass.
Oh, pity the bigots who scream and yell

And scribble curses they misspell,
Whose bowels are ever letting gas,
So they can't help the way they smell.

Their daily life's a form of hell
With test upon test they'll never pass.
Pity the bigots who scream and yell,

And offer them a looking glass
Inscribed, in Hebrew, *I'm an ass.*
Pity the bigots who scream and yell
And cannot help the way they smell.

Systems of Mourning

The Irish hire keeners, the English mutes.
Some hobbyists will bronze the loved one's boots.

Revival theaters devote entire weeks
To proofs that Elvis Lives and Garbo Speaks.

Vikings consign their chieftains to the waves,
And Amy Clampitt visits famous graves.

Sorrowing bees return to ruined hives,
And Hindus burn their neighbors' grieving wives.

A dog will mourn his master like a serf
By pissing on the dear departed's turf.

Some weep in silence, others cry out loud,
And Susan Cheever sells her father's shroud.

In a Time of Plagues

Deer reck not of the hunting season.
    Sheep can't imagine shepherd's pie.
Smokers scorn the voice of reason.
    No one knows the day he'll die.

Gays there were who never heeded
    All the headlines about AIDS.
Drinkers drank, and still they speeded.
    Every color finally fades.

Power lines are thought to kill
    People who live too close by.
Look at your electric bill,
    Then think about the day you'll die.

No life's secure: oaks may defy
    Death for a century, but they,
Too, in the course of time must die.
    Timor mortis conturbat me.

A War Memorial

The while they scrambled to escape
    The consequences of their crimes –
Torture, pillage, murder, rape,
    According to *The Times* –

Allah the Merciless prepared
    The banquet destined for Iraq.
'Let no expense, or life, be spared,'
    He bade. 'And now, attack!'

For fifty miles and four lanes wide
    The hulks of trucks and gutted cars
Still fill the highway where they died
    Huzzahing, 'Victory is ours!'

Waking Early New Year's Day, Without a Hangover

Look at the map and tell me where
A conscious mind would not despair.
In Poland? Palestine? Peru?
In Angkor Wat? In Timbuktu?
Twist as you will upon the grid
Of North, South, East, and West, amid
Whatever fleshpots Rome may boast,
Or safe at home with buttered toast,
At last it all comes down to this –
The world's too big for bombs to miss,
The law too weak, the door too wide
To forestall every suicide.
While there are motive, means, and time
There will, as sure as death, be crime.

Our hope must be that those who've got
The right, or guns, to have us shot
Will set a limit to their catch
And feel no need to fire the thatch;
That just as long as power buys
Good opera seats and alibis
The guilty rich will be content
Still to convene their Parliament,
Still to resist the urge to wreak
Some vengeance on their heirs, the meek.
How like the thief's benign reprieve,
Who'd spare our lives and only thieve.
So long as we do not protest
We even may enjoy the jest.
This is the social contract we
In A.D. 1983
Must live by if we mean to live,
Committing sins we can't forgive
With every coffee bean we grind,

And every heart, and every mind.
(For surely if you've wit to trace
A line of logic through this lace
Of verses, you're among the few
Who're well- or well-enough-to-do
And can't too bitterly complain:
For thoughtful minds are free of pain
To the degree that they can think
And alchemize their thoughts to ink.
Happy the man who can declare
His angst with any savoir faire.
More happy still if he repine
Over a five-buck jug of wine.)

How swiftly, ably fear deflects
The squeamish eye away from texts
So dire toward each bright ad's plea
For booze and equanimity.
Or is it rather tyranny
Internalized that turns the eye
And tunes the slavish tongue to praise
Our meted lengths of rope and days?
Laud we the gods, for yet we breathe,
And hang in heaven a smoky wreath
Of thanks for yielding yet a year
More to the time we're sentenced here.
Between the jailer and the jailed
There's no hope lost. The god that failed
To intervene at Buchenwald
Will not decide to be appalled
At infamies that shall be nameless.
That god is dead, and history aimless.

Enough of pealing New Year's chimes.
I want my coffee and *The Times*.

Jerusalem Recaptured

Los cries, 'Obey my voice & never deviate from my will
And I will be merciful to thee! be thou invisible to all
To whom I make thee invisible, but chief to my own Children.
O Spectre of Urthona!'
     – WILLIAM BLAKE, *Jerusalem*

Albion! of thy sons and daughters, once verdant fields
And frolic cities, what can be sung in choirs echoic? Or thine,
Oosa, co-heir and tardy drudge, now that thy mills
Stand lorn and ungolden that once were clamorous
With all the oaths and lusts of Toyle? Bereft art thou,
As when, at noon, unnoticed, outside the blasted Temple wall,
Homeless Goofus begs for quarters: Bereft, yet necessary
To sorry Newscasters omniscient, whose woeful stories stir
The sons of Toyle, their daughters equally, more ware of Woe
Yet to weave and weld, as in the days of Albion's eld.
What's to be hoped, or dreaded more, when each tee-shirt,
On each misshapen chest, cries to eyes that still can see:
Alas, look all about yourselves and dare to speak the truth!
We weep and laugh and cannot but despair. Number us,
Record our spare simplicities, as when Kepler the proud
    Astronomer
Sizes the stars and makes their stories ours, which else
Are recordless.

         Then from her Beautyrest arose Magnifica
And answer'd: 'The Neighborhoods of Paradise are seven
In number. The first is Gramercy; the second Tudor City,
Where the taut cords of elevators bind Albion's thews; third
Is the tutued ballerina Loisaida, round of leg;
Fourth Flushing, Queens; the other names are on my secret
Rolodex.' She dressed and talced and flew away
In a Metropolitan Transportation Authority helicopter,
And the roar of the rotors was as the whirlwind

Of Schizophrenia or the howling of the Society of Friends,
Distraught for Albion's children. See here on the third page
Of today's Times: the Courts condemn Ezra Baxter of the Bronx
For distributing clean needles! Where do the grapefruits come from
    stacked
In cannonball pyramids in the produce department of the A & P?
And whence this single coffeebean precious to me
As the jewelries of Paloma Picasso? Riddles!
Oh, I am sick, there is a Blister on my heel, and I must take
Synthroid for a hypothyroid condition, yet look at the Valleys of
    Duchess County
And examine Westchester's Groves, and there is an Equality
Of Suffering. Albion and Oosa lie side by side, one snoring,
T'other sleepless, and the sable wings of midnight, Eastern
Daylight Savings Time, spread wide across their Dreams &
    Medications.

Ding-a-ling-a-ling! Ding-a-ling-a-ling! Do not touch Pause
But rouse thyself instanter, O Somnolence of Albion!
Anoint thy limbs, lissome Oosa, with balm of aloe
And Liquid Ivory. Throw off thy sheets, for History sounds
Its hellish din in bed & torture chamber, meadow & oil field,
Where doubled-headed Exxon crunches Albion's numbers. Awake!
Stir, Oosa, thy Quaker Oats! One head, turned east,
Already blinks its mucused single Orb; t'other
Murmurs as though in dazey sleep commanding teams
Of corporate tax accountants, sharkskin-suited sneaky minions
Of Multinational Inc. Exxon rises, and the sun also,
And History's afoot, unfurling gassy banners
Of stinking hydrocarbons, nuclear waste, pollution piled
Upon pollution, self-compounding. He wipes the ochrous crust
From his dull eye and snorts bituminous phlegm from clotted nares.
Then in a dulcet tenor he sings advertisements, and e'en the snows
Of chill Antarctica melt before the melody, the Ozone
Opening a hole, and punishing sunlight streaming through.
O Albion, take heed: the digits flicker on thy dials,

Whilst still thou drowsest beside fair Oosa fast asleep.
Hearken to the hands that knock & scrabble at the latch!
Heed the winged words of Poesy while she has utterance yet.

At last Albion and Oosa wake, commute to work, commence
Their daily Grind, and the Millwheels of the GNP engage,
Gear into Gear, the glitt'ring necklaces of Toyle, a maze
Of spinnings, whirlings, throbs & pulses, muscle & machine,
Girding the bosom of the polity with Quickways and major
     arteries.
Revivified Moolah, lovely & mysterious, streams invisible
Though the trembling fingers of Nasdaq and Amex.
'Caress me,' she croons, 'and comb my long golden hair.
Braid it with silver bangles; employ for each dainty foot
Its own podiatrist; bankrupt an Iowa hamlet each time
I think of raspberries in a Spode raspberry bowl.
Nothing is too good for me. Imelda & Leona are my handmaids,
And Nancy draws breath only to sweep the crumbs from the fable
That is my tablecloth. Let Oosa join me now in Congress
Unforbidden. Let her bring to my banquet a Chalice
Brimming with her spouse's blood, for all men must toast me
With such sweet Liqueur, by which all Virtue is engend'red:
The Virtue to kill or be killed, the Virtue of Flowerly Joy,
Which neither toyles nor spins, but sucks up Minerals
From the soil and grows large and waxes in beauty & swells with
     Increase
Until the Berry hangs upon the bending stem, pendulous and
     satisfied.'

Thus spake luxurious Moolah, to whom, with hesitations
And candor incomplete, Albion replies: 'Fair art thy fingertips,
And crimson thy lacquered Nails, O Glamor Imperial.
All men pay the Taxes thou imposest, none are exempt;
The very corpses on their gibbets empty their pockets
Into thy coffers. To honor thee the toddlers of Brooklyn push
     crack,

And labor unremitting breaks their mother's back. To honor thee
Poesy obscures her sense, in maund'ring mazes lost,
Clutching the while her reticule of Tenures and Preferments.
To honor thee our citizens compete in Tournaments of Cruelty,
They cheer as Orphans beat each other into insensibility
And halftime harlots instruct how to chant their names & wages.
These honors all are thine, yet may not I keep some little morsel
Of what's mine? This coffeebean perhaps?' He held it up, and
Moolah laughed & grabbed, and cracked it with her golden teeth
And spit it to the floor & ground it beneath her golden heel
And sighed, and signaled to her Chancellor Philosophy
To speak for her, which in this wise he did:

                                        'O reckless Albion,
Thus to expose the little thing you love; the shell or feather,
The matchless stocking, the unpaired glove. Can you suppose
The Lions of Predation can ignore the Mites of Penury?
While Goofus has a peppercorn of self-esteem, while there remains
A kernel still unpopped at the bottom of Jolly Time's bag,
While still a minute can be syphoned from thy balance
To Moolah's immeasurable Vaults, thou shalt be pauperized &
    squeezed.
Yeah, and thy children too, heirs of Insolvency, whom Moolah
Derisory shall dress in rags of Fashion & send to Universities.
Nothing shall escape her grasp if she desires it;
We are her prawns & appetizers.'

This hearing, Albion grieves, and Oosa, malingering in the employee
Washroom, makes sad lament, not for the bean but for the world
Within the bean, for all Futurity. Oosa foresees that Albion's
Sons shall leave no progeny, and her daughters wither & spoil
Like the Lawns of Gladness beneath the Canopy of Extinction.
Albion, console her! for she is comfortless and full of dread.

V

The Great Outdoors

The Return to Nature

I

Here I am, wood nymphs, obedient
To your imperious demand
To spend my summer in your land.
Besides, it is expedient
At times to put the world on Hold
And wander off to realms where gold
Is just a metaphor. So here as lamb
Reporting to its bleating dam
I am, notebook in hand, where mushrooms
Rhyme to each other on a dead log
And birds quite literally tweet.
Only a buzzsaw spoils the sweetness
Of the view. (No offense, Dryads, to you.
I might have gone farther from home
To find some still lonesomer bog,
But buzzsaws would have been there, too.)

★

But look, you have proven me wrong:
I had only to follow the gleam
Of your mid-morning lamps up a stream
And over some scree, and behold I have found
Your twelve-foot-high, one-hundred-fifty-foot long,
Moss-hung, immemorial grotto.
A Midsummer-Night's Dream
Is accurate. There *are* fairy flies
That haunt these enchanted grounds.
Dryads, I honor your shrine, and hang
Upon its massive, mossy frieze
This preliminary motto:
The gods are just, though hard to please,
And seldom if ever play Lotto.

As I linger here, still out of breath,
I am put in mind of death,
That worst and best of reasons
For leading a more strenuous life.
Meanwhile, clinging to the cliff,
Some doughty Protestant pines
Refuse to cede to my worry of 'If
There be works but no grace . . .'
For their roots are fixed like pitons in the face
Of the rock and won't yield to anything
Less than a bolt of lightning.
All those old chestnuts, the pines declare,
That celebrate hardship and glorify strife,
Are right as rain. Life is not vain,
Though poets may be. Only dare
And you'll succeed. Even as the pines berate me,
I'm up, with my imaginary Alpenstock,
Mounting the heights above the Muses' fane
To where rhododendrons await me.

⋆

I praise the goddess who split
This rock to be my writing desk
And sent a welcoming committee
Of polyrhythmic jays. The profusion
Of flowers – sublime!
It's just what I was looking tor,
Except . . . I think I'm lost.

⋆

But back I skidoodled, even so,
A crow-flight right to our back door,
Detouring only for a branch
Of pink blooms that have proven not
To be rhododendrons but guess what?

Bay laurels! *Non sum dignus*, darling Muses.
And yet . . . it is a shrub that has its uses.

II

Now, the next day, or evening to be
Accurate, my imagination is a boat
Steering between the Scylla of Keats
And the Charybdis of Auden, a polarity
Inadvertently brought about
By exigencies of packing.
Not hard to see which of the two
Poets-in-residence is winning
Tonight, luring my small craft ever nearer
His mind-monopolizing maw. Yet who,
Knowing a whirlpool in the neighborhood,
Could resist a peek? Then — *Schloop!* —
It's too late, your little sloop
Has been assimilated to his sea.
As for our other bard, *tant pis*:
Tomorrow I'll venture a draught of the true,
The blushful Hippocrene again, and every day
Until the summer's at an end, renewing
My vows of truth-in-beauty
In the freshets of John Keats
(And in, of course, your courses, Muses, too).

    ★

Meanwhile my boat is merely drunk, riot drowned,
And the light that leads me kindly, not blinding.
If I were now to need reminding,
My erratic wind-up alarm should do the trick
(As it just did). Reminding me of what?
Some duty? Some debt?

Of something tax-related anyhow; just what, I forget.
This, if I haven't already explained, is the stream
Of my consciousness, neither more nor less,
Whereon *mon beateau, ma ivresse,*
Glides gently down the stream of –
Ah, but I've already rhymed to that.
Oh Keats – dear, dead, too little read,
Too little dreaded friend, and you, dear Auden, too –
There is nothing, *nothing* I wouldn't do
To have your grasp(s) of all that makes the world
Seem strange, to know as surely as both of you
Why laurels bloom and verities are ever true.

Monday, June 13

III

It's Tuesday night, though there's still sunlight,
And if it weren't for my left hip's
Acting up, I'd be home in Homeostatisville.
But I didn't today (tomorrow I will)
Visit you, Muses, up on your hill.
In lieu whereof I took the briefest of dips
In the stream, Pine Kill, after the drive
Back from – where was it? – oh yes, Monroe.
And though I'm tired, I've wheels to show
And anywhere I want to I can go
So long as I stay within the local area.
Thus pooped, Muses, excuse me if I don't tarry a
While longer *tête-à-tête.* A mystery now, and then
To bed. The car? A Skylark. Bronze. '77.
Tired as I am, I feel I'm in heaven!
Not on account of the Buick; it's you,
Dear nymphs, and the stream, and the view.

Tuesday, June 14

IV

Good as my word, I've been to their shrine
And hauled off years of dry deadwood,
Clearing the aisles of branch and vine,
Forming vistas, framing views,
Until (how long it took I couldn't say:
My watch stopped working Saturday)
It looked as a nymphaeum should
And I was sweating like a sluice.
So Adam worked in Paradise –
Not for a living (he needed no wage,
For lunch was free in that Golden Age)
But just for love of the native gneiss.

Wednesday, June 15

V

This is no diary, but it must be explained
How the momentum of daily life's maintained,
For I could no more go three months alone –
No mail, not knowing who had tried to phone –
Than sail, *tout seul*, from Maine to Port-au-Prince.
So, lacking other subsidies or grants,
Here's how it's done: Charlie shuttles back
And forth between the city and our shack
Beside Pine Kill with the requisite caffeines
Of news, reviews, due bills, and coffee beans.
He came last night; today we drove to Ellenville
And did the laundry. Now, with time to kill,
I took (I thought) the path toward your fane
And found (so quickly lost) what bones remain
Of what had been (a year ago?) a deer
(His antlers taken as a souvenir):
Six ribs, some vertebrae, the jaws torn loose
But still close by the plundered skull. O Muse,

Am I perhaps not lost? Is *this* your shrine —
This shambles rain has brimmed and redesigned?
Where is the garden Adam yesterday
Made neat and trim in post-lapsarian play?
On higher ground, no doubt; this basin but
The deepest widest passage of the cut
I cross each day to reach our realm of make-
Believe. What next, my Muse — a rattlesnake?
Wiser I'd been tonight if I'd remained in
The cabin I was rained (no, make that 'reined') in.

Thursday, June 16

VI

The wide consensus of the fallen pines
Is that the steepest path's the quickest to the top,
An ethical position they maintain
Even as mossy logs. Yet look at our unyielding
Pilgrim Fathers as they attain to that top:
We find them falling all over each other,
Sprawling on the stronger maples, recumbent
On the here-so-much-more-substantial rocks,
Bashing the poor resilient birches (who, even so,
Enjoy, together with the laurels, a clear plurality).
It's as though they'd given up on being pines
Marshalled up the slopes in paramilitary lines
And let the birches and the laurels take over,
As all these blossoms seem to say
They deserve to. Democracy! The bees agree
(Though they don't forego some interest in me),
And the first real songbird I've heard up here
Repeats the bees' message loud and clear:
Hail to the sun and the level plain!
Hail to easeful life and gentle rain!
Hail to hives and the nests of birds!
Hail to the flowers and the words

The spirit of these woods inspires –
And hail to death and forest fires!
A song with which these pines nor me
Can quite whole-heartedly agree.

Friday, June 17

VII

The seventh, and a day if not of rest
At least of closure. As in 'Close your
Books, class. Today we have a test.'
A test! And yesterday, descending
From the summit, I lost, or thought
I lost, my Mark Cross pen, a present
Infinite Christmases ago from Charlie.
'Oh no!' I cried – then wondered if
My Muses had extracted it in payment
For their manifold largesse, the which
In prelude to a proper thank-you
I here enumerate (Ye Nymphs and Dryads,
Bend your ears!): Item, one novel resumed
After a lapse of several years; Item, another
Newly conceived, a sequel of sorts to *Clara Reeve*;
Item, this poem for what it's worth; Item, a dream,
The night before last, from which I woke at 2 a.m.
To stumble down from the sleeping loft and scrawl
The verses of the song my dream-self sang,
A Black Mass version of the big finale
In which Gene Kelly salutes Tin Pan Alley
And the Great White Way. This is not the moment
To repeat those lyrics, but it's rare for the rhymes
Of a dream to bear looking at in the light of day –
And these were okay. What I'm saying,
Woodland Muses, is that you've really got
My juices flowing, and if the price for that
Must be my pen, well then, I'll pay. But then

This morning – here's the kicker – when I'd come home,
After an after-breakfast search along the path
Beside the stream where I remembered
Bending down to marvel at a scattering
Of sylvan oyster shells and to gather specimens
For a backyard mycological preserve and where
It seemed most logical I might have lost my pen,
There – that's to say here – on my desk
It was. And I could swear it wasn't here last night!
And Charlie swears too, by the laurels on the table
(Charlie, who wouldn't lie if he were able),
That he didn't find it and plant it there.
Which means it must have come from you, the geniuses
Of the place. So, Muses, that is why,
As I end my song, it is of thee I sing –
To thee I offer thanks for everything.

Saturday, June 18

Sylvan Marriage

a Rustic Epithalamion

Here stand the oaks their acorn-spangled ground,
Saluting the mountain, presenting it a crown;
Here the flowery ladies of the court,
The laurels and lesser bushes, sport,
Devising bright, attractive ways
To bring Sir Honeybee to graze;
And here, attentive but unseen,
A solitary hermit clad in green
Remarks the morals and manners of this throng
And turns the lot of it into his song.

O hear, he sings, *the lesson of the field,*
The message by each bud concealed!
Those who marry must know this:
There's reckless danger in a kiss.
The honeycomb and sweets inside
Are there because some petals died.
Unless a blossom sacrifice its youth,
Fruit shall not weight the boughs with harvest truth.

See then that every bridal gown,
Whether of country or the town,
Is decked in heraldries of the May.
Then let the droning pipers play.
Let blossomed branches strew the hall
And decorate each pew and stall.
So may the couple better understand
The golden oaths exchanged from hand to hand.

Experience proves, the sage went on,
That Nature loves to breed and spawn,
To bear new seed, to fruit and whelp,
And we must do our best to help.

Accept, therefore, beloved pair,
The strict necessity of despair –
But celebrate, while still these laurels bloom,
The sweet occasion of your mutual doom.

Birdsong Interpreted

Scuse me? Scuse M? This is *my* territory.
Didja hear what I said? I said, Go away!
No trespassing! Vamoose! Amscray!
Everything was hunky-dory
Till *you* disturbed the eco-balance.
I homestead here and you're Jack Palance
Terrorizing godly folk.
Leave! or I will have a stroke.
I will! I kid you not. I'll sing
My heart out, pop a valve, expire:
This nest will be my funeral pyre.
I'm warning you: if songs could sting,
If trills could kill, my dear sweet thing,
You wouldn't linger longer here.
Jug jug, pu-whee! – now, disappear!

Nightmare on Elm Street

The elms looked down, struck by the fact,
As by an ax, of the destruction wrought
All about them. The local, nest-dwelling
Giant hairless squirrels were dying off,
Limbs wizening, stomachs bloating up,
Livers sickening, brains on the blink.
The sick ones were going at a faster rate
Than they were being replaced by new growth.
Soon, by the elms' calculations,
The entire species would be extinct. A pity,
For they had provided a constant source
Of wonder, what with their foolish fear
Of sunlight, and their nightly worship
At glowing shrines, each a miniature sun.
There by the shrines' pallid effulgence
They would caress the desiccated tissues
Of mummified trees – a horrid rite
But, for the elms, unable to imagine
A similar fate befalling themselves, an act
Imbued with romance. When they were gone
The neighborhood would never be the same.
But what were the elms to do? Immortal
Themselves, they were as powerless
As the gods of high Olympus to confer
Immortality on those they loved.

The Dirt and the Willow

all summer long
while other trees
reached for more
light the willow
unfurled streamers
down into its own
streetwise shade
lower and slower
until the silvery
tip of its lowest
leaf had reached
the limit set to
its inverted growth:
dirt's intractable
horizontality

Enough it thought
if willows think
these accretions
are taking me
nowhere
        Whereupon
it came to its annual
decision to drop
everything it was
doing and die
          Just try
the dirt wisecracked
not unkindly but
the willow was
aquiver with indignant
self-pity and wouldn't
sit still for such 'sitcom
optimism'

It's easy
for tombs to talk
about eternal recurrence
to equate one string
of proteins with another
the wailing child
and the ailing mother
tombs have nothing
to lose   oh what's the use
you'll never understand

On the contrary said the dirt
that's what I do best
now why don't you just rest

Coming To

'Mountain,' he said,
        taking the tone
of one familiar with mountains
        (which was not his own),
'Mountain, you've changed.'

The mountain sighed. It had no time
        for these vacationers
who rent a cottage for two weeks in June
and expect to be treated like Ammons
        or Thoreau.
        'Go away,'
said the mountain. 'It's going to rain.'

        An obvious lie:
        the sky was blue.

He sat on a rock, took out his notebook,
        thought.
        *The mountain is falling
to pieces*, he wrote, *and so am I.*
        He considered adding
        the adverb 'slowly'.
He tried to imagine the manner
        in which a mountain
        might write poems.
It would be like Gertrude Stein
        with repeated phrases
        undergoing
minimal variations of tone and inflection
        as did the hemlocks
        and mosses on the rocks.

'Mountains,' the mountain commented
disdainfully, 'wouldn't write poems.'
      But then as though
      in contradiction
some very liquid-voiced kind of bird
asserted its territorial claims
      in what sounded
      to the listener
sitting there exactly like music.

No! he thought. No, not like Gertrude Stein:
but like Gary Snyder with a free open flowing
line and a willingness to take on all the big themes,
      love, death, duty,
      beauty, truth,
freedom . . . Freedom especially.

'Actually,' said the mountain, 'what we are
      mostly interested in
      talking about
is old movies. The drive-ins
have made an enormous difference up here.
      Have you seen *Beau Geste*?'

'I didn't come all the way to Sullivan County
and climb to such a height to entertain
      nostalgia for Gary Cooper.
      Anyhow,
you must be suffering from senile dementia:
Beau Geste hasn't played anywhere for years.'

      'I love the way,'
      the mountain went on,
'a movie instantly becomes part of the landscape.
That's a theme that has yet to find its Manet,
      much less its Michelangelo.'

'Since when,' the visitor waxed indignant,
'do mountains talk of Michelangelo!'

'You'd be surprised what mountains know.
        Mountains aren't dumb.'

        'Indeed – I see
they can be downright garrulous.

'You have to visit them at home,'
        it rambled on,
        'see what they value,
what they can do without. Mountains like
a variety of textures, large patterns,
        a telling detail,
        and then,
when least expected, a precipice,
a recent skeleton along the path,
        or best of all,
        this – the laurel-crowned
summit of the slope. *There's* truth
and beauty for you. That's what's possible.
        And it's what you
        must learn to do.'

How true, concurred the visitor. How very true.

Brief Lives

Between the inkling and the act,
    the fancy and the brutal fact,

Between the blossom and the berry,
    the broken hymen and the bursting sac,

There intervenes a season
    seemingly dry –

The pistil swollen, russet-red,
    the stamen desiccated –

And this is the reason
    the heart may die

Before its time, believing the lie
    of the petal gone black,

The soil gone dry, only aware
    of its thirst, its needs,

Forgetful of its thrusting roots,
    its airborne seeds

Already swelling and ready to split
    their brevity to wit.

The Mushrooms' Salon

The mushrooms are busy showing samples to the trees:
'Will it be russet, M'am, or one of these?'

The trees confer. The willows choose a lemon rinse.
The maples opt for Ultra-Orange. The grave oaks wince.

A plump and speckled mushroom minces to the oaks:
'Oh, M'am, that's not for you! These maples have their jokes,

But you're more *serious*. Now here's a Tawny Brown
That will take you absolutely anywhere in town.'

'Thank you, my dear mushroom. Yes, that's just the thing
To tide me over till I can come back in the spring.'

The Last Shows of Summer

Most of the first hits of summer are dead
Or at least have lost their legs:
The leaves of the rhododendrons yellow
As squash; the softer, water-loving flowers
Retired from the field, readying for HBO.
Only *The Return of the Jedi* still hangs on –
And probably will survive, like holly
In a hedgerow, till Christmas – despite
The fact that no one seems to be enjoying it.
Well, what of that. We haven't reached
Labor Day yet. August's last contenders
Are already warming up: some marvelous new
Mushrooms, spreads of goldenrod, huge
Black bugs to whet the appetites of all
Insectivores. Oh, the crowds are out there,
Hungry as ever. It's up to Hollywood now
To pop some popcorn and bring in the sheaves.

September

Slice the earth anywhere
& like a plumcake it yields
one thumbful after another
of late estival yumminess
yams & more yams, tuberous
boobs of a subterranean
Cybele discovering herself
fan by fan, shovel by shovel
to the insatiable gaze
of the whistling, worshipful
clods, who call aloud the litanies
of cookbook & bawdry
Crisp potatoskins, steamed ears
of corn, ripe tomatoes steeped
in virgin olive oil
The votive ovens glow like flesh
Our hearts & mouths are full
of praise & sweet potatoes

October

Without the fables of these falling leaves
How would we know how to die? Living on
The veldt we would have to imagine ourselves
Falling prey to lions, praying to leonine gods,
Devourers of our kind. Heaven forbid. Better
To give lip service to the myths of these
More temperate climes, the Aurora of autumn,
April's putative cruelty, June's spoonfuls
Of ripe berries. Then if our poets cry
Ashes, ashes, all fall down, we have been
Fortified, inoculated, preserved
Against the day we would have come, if not
To dust, to some similar dismal
Conclusion. But we don't. We continue
Living, in a manner of speaking, the lives
We have agreed to live, just like these
Deciduous trees, whose leaves we have learned
To make our teas from. We rustle
In the breeze and take out dying falls,
But we are seasonal, our hours and our days
Recurring, even as the South Pole dies,
Even as we tell ourselves these lies.

Indian Spring

When fate is kind, it falls at Christmas,
The spring of winter, Indian Spring –
Then every Olds and Camarro
Rejoices in a new two-tone snowjob
And every heart is glad to remember
The neanderthal past when we were all
Snowbound south of the glaciers, evolving
An appropriate genetic response, a child
Sturdier than ourselves. The tingle
Of that hope and dread still lingers
In our blood, to bloom each Indian Spring
Into these – these barbaric Christmas trees
We annually erect to celebrate
The felicitous continuity between then
And now, that Now again controlled
By snow. Snow, beautiful soft white
Snow – and cruel, world-burying snow, too;
It all depends on one's point of view.
Not everyone develops the knack
Of surviving the true winter ahead,
All those days you'll wish you were dead.
But no, not really, that's not so:
You'll wish you were alive but in another hemisphere,
If not of this earth, then of a mind
That can construe the embers' shadows
On the cave's bare walls as reindeer
Approaching your dwelling with blessings of meat
And whatever other good things to eat
The season affords. O the benison
Of rare venison, the comfort of Southern Comfort
And home-brewed mead! When needs are satisfied
And hearths are fueled, we are as those squirrels
We imagine on our Christmas cards, the privileged
Squirrels of well-connected parks,

Where all winter long the little darlings
Scamper through their allegories
Of hunger daily appeased; unlike in that
The guilty derelicts who witness these same antics
With far other thoughts, thoughts, surely,
Of death, maledictions on a scheme of things
That allows snow, and misery, and the ironic
Reflection that even the songs
Of birds are a defense of nests. But not,
No, not yet, our Christmas carols:
They yet maintain the right of what's alive
To life – despite the cold, despite
Everything. For they share the wisdom
Of Indian Spring, which knows, along
With us, that life revives, that even
The most tenuous houseplant left
Unprovided, even *it* survives,
And the world *is* loveable, and the days do
Gradually lengthen after the solstice
And life goes on. Life does go on.

Rocks on a Winter Evening

These boulders are the turds the glaciers dropped
On their precipitate northbound retreat;
Flushed down the mountainside, they finally stopped
Beside this frozen stream, where they repeat
Each snowy night the self-same dream of flight
North to the heaven of the coprolite.

Theseus to Hippolyta

The imperative demands of nature that we share
With the wasp, the ocelot and the bear,
Should serve to remind us that a spade
Is a spade, and men and women both are made
Upon the self-same armature, whence
Their capabilities for innocence
And certain doom.
Life is a loom
Whereon a foolishness of feathers
Is warp to woof of shifting weathers.
The egret plumes himself upon his dance
And leaves his wide posterity to chance.
Each molecule
Has been to school
And learned the rudiments of Rock and Roll.
See where Primavera bears the scroll
Of all the flowers Eve has named: the Rose,
The Buttercup, the Daisy, Plato's Nose,
And, here at home,
The Rhyming Poem,
A bloom that's fair as it is rare
(Thou wear'st it sometimes in thy hair).
Sweet is its nectar as Nutra-Sweet,
Yet nourishing as durum wheat.
O fair Hippolyta, thou art that Poem,
And on thy breast I'd make my home.

Songs of the Rooftops

I PLATO'S SONG

When lovely Phyllis licks my ear
No more am I an ordinary cat:
I breathe another atmosphere
And move through jungles odorous and dim,
A silence following – the silence of the fear
My form commands. I grow so heavy that
Branches bend double as I leap from limb
To limb. I spy my prey – I slither near –
Phyllis, sweetest, do you hear? –
I crouch – I spring! – Phyllis! Phyllis, I adore
You! Why at just this moment must she always disappear?

I'm left alone with nothing more
Than these bowls of milk and meatless bones
That are replenished every night
Outside the giants' awful cave –
Bowls of milk and meatless bones
And longing sighs and anguished groans.
O love! O hunger! O lost delight!
At first you tempt and then enslave
Even the proudest appetite.
Phyllis? Fairest Phyllis? Phyllis dear?
Please, O please, O please come here.

2 PHYLLIS'S SONG

The sun is out and seems to burn
Through fur and flesh into the purring soul
Itself. Why doesn't Plato ever learn
The art of basking?
Why must there always be a goal?
There is his bowl:
It's almost full. Why is he forever asking
More from life, and me, than life
Or I are pleased to give?
What a bore to be a wife
To someone who will not simply live
His life from day to day
And drink his milk and draw his pay,
Keeping dry within a box
If it should rain (though I doubt
It means to rain today),
And maintaining an orthodox
View. That is all one needs to do.
That is what life's all about.
I wish you'd listen, Plato, when I talk to you.

The Squirrel

His charm in begging can exceed
Even his egregious greed.

He lifts his paws, he glints his eyes;
He asks so little, looks so wise.

Let all good children act as he
And families shall know harmony.

Dialogue with a Spider

In every weather, wet or dry,
How tensely you anticipate
The serendipitous but certain fly.
To us what seems mere happenchance
To you is sweet mosquito pie
And destined by the laws of Fate
To be your partner in the dance
Of your demand and its supply.

Where's the error in such a plan?
If flies are born, then flies must die.
This swamp would be a churning hell
Of hungry gnats, were 't not for I.
Did not the godly Son of Man
Eat lamb — and so elect to die?
You *have been known to buy and sell —*
But hush, here comes another fly.

The Chameleon and the Butterfly

'I have been compared to many things,'
the butterfly said, settling down comfortably
beside an old chameleon, 'but never more aptly than just now
when I was likened to the eyes of that young lady there.'

The chameleon's eyes darted to the bushes where
a young man was romancing a young woman.
'Her eyes are spherical,' the chameleon objected,
'and *you* are wafer-thin.'

                       The butterfly gave its wings
a little flutter and spread a spritz of spit on its antennae:
'It is the way her glance (he told her) rests on his face —
like that butterfly (meaning me) that has lighted on the nose
of that licheny Minerva (that's who that statue is, you know),
at once so goldenly bold (his words, not mine) and so oblivious.'

'Oblivious?' the chameleon blinked. 'Of whom?'
But the butterfly had flown off, so as not to be eaten.

The Hawk and the Metaphor

A sharp-eyed hawk and a just metaphor;

A well-ornamented metaphor,
                   a well-balanced hawk;

A hawk soaring on the wind,
                   a metaphor with its feet on the ground;

A hawk-eyed metaphor aloft,
                   scanning the ground for what hawks like –

            tender young metaphors in their nests,
            timid metaphors burrowing into the earth,
            slow-writhing metaphors beyond the realm of
                 Consciousness as we understand it;

A metaphorical hawk preening
                   in a pediment, august, the perfect predator;

That's what I like: eye like a hawk; I like a metaphor.

Remarks Concerning the Fitness of All Things

How wonderfully apt our Maker's Plan,
Who crafted Matter for the use of Man;
Breath'd Oxygen into th' ambient Air
In measured Quantities that all might share;
Spread out the Oceans to their very Shores
And framed firm Apples on their ample Cores;
Created Night as foil to bustling Day –
Dark Night, when all our Toys are put away –
And bade bright Phoebus, when the Night was done,
At once his bold diurnal Course to run;
Who legislated Gravity's strict Laws,
Decree'd for each Effect its needful Cause;
Maintains the Stars in their Trajectories,
And comforts parsons in their rectories.

Mahler's 8th

Veni! it begins. *Veni, Creator*
Spiritus! Because it always seems to do
The job, I'm stingy with my talisman.
Romeo and Juliet will jump-start me
Most days. Mahler's 8th is for emergencies,
When nothing less than heaven's massed chorus
Will serve the purpose.
                He went each summer
To the mountains, high as he could get, and wrote
A symphony. So I recall having read
And do believe. High altitudes have that effect.
Even the Poconos, so much lower than
The Alps, exert an influence, and I am
Feeling it. Again.
             And again the wood thrush
That haunts my rented glade insists I am,
As he, the Spirit's willing slave. He sings,
Exactly as the Field Guide says, *Ee-o-lay*
(With occasional, distinctive, guttural notes)
And so much else besides, flutelike and
Rounder than other thrushes, and I awake
At four a.m. and can't go back to sleep
For the glory of it.
             Why does the wood thrush
Sing such songs, while other birds still sleep? –
Unless it is he sings because there's music
In him. Not some territorial claim,
Not some dumb desire, but an instinct co-equal
With ours, and no less unaccountable,
To achieve beauty and inhabit it.

What that music may mean he knows no more
Than me or John Keats or John Keats' nightingale
Or Mahler on his mountaintop. We all
Are equal in our innocence. The dawn
Glimmers and we respond in kind.
                              It's six
p.m., and that amazing bird is still at it.

Some recent poetry from Anvil

Tony Connor
Things Unsaid
SELECTED POEMS 1960–2005

Jibanananda Das
Bengal the Beautiful
TRANSLATED BY JOE WINTER

Michael Hamburger
Circling the Square

Donald Justice
Collected Poems
(Not for sale in the USA)

Stanley Moss
Songs of Imperfection

Oktay Rifat
Poems of Oktay Rifat
TRANSLATED BY RUTH CHRISTIE
AND RICHARD McKANE

Georg Trakl
The Poems of Georg Trakl
TRANSLATED BY MARGITT LEHBERT

www.anvilpresspoetry.com